Stirred - Not Shaken

The Dry Martini

Was th[illegible]ented in Paris? London[illegible] City?

When w[illegible] the Dry Martini first served? And by whom?

What is the oldest Dry Martini story?

Do you know how to make the perfect Dry Martini?

What did W. C. Fields say when they doctored his favourite tipple?

Why was a Gibson so named? – and what the heck is a Murphy?

These are the questions, among many others, which John Doxat answers in *Stirred – Not Shaken.* In this irresistible blend of wit and wisdom he covers every aspect of the greatest cocktail ever devised, which has since the early years of this century been the favourite of a wide range of well-known characters, from John D. Rockefeller (for whom it was apparently invented) to James Bond. You don't even have to like the Dry Martinis to be entertained by John Doxat's special mix. History, mystery, fact, fiction, folklore, jokelore – it's all in *Stirred – Not shaken,* the first truly international book about the Dry Martini.

As Kingsley Amis says in his Aperitif to the book,

> John Doxat has all the qualifications needed by a writer on drink: knowledge, experience (plenty of that), the practical approach, an eye for the revealing anecdote or out-of-the-way fact, spontaneous wit, and more. Who is better fitted to tackle the subject of this book than a man whose style is clear, dry, cool, flavoursome and balanced, all combining to produce a comfortable glow in the consumer?

The Compleat Martinian

Stirred–Not Shaken

The Dry Martini

JOHN DOXAT

With an Aperitif by Kingsley Amis

Hutchinson Benham, London

Also by John Doxat

Drinks and Drinking

Booth's Handbook of Cocktails
and Mixed Drinks
The Book of Drinking

Hutchinson Benham Ltd
3 Fitzroy Square, London W1

An imprint of the Hutchinson Group

London Melbourne Sydney Auckland
Wellington Johannesburg and agencies
throughout the world

First published 1976

Designed and produced by Hutchinson Benham
Printed in Great Britain by litho by The Anchor Press Ltd
and bound by Wm Brendon & Son Ltd
both of Tiptree, Essex

ISBN 0 09 127661 6

Dedication

It has been reported that a celebrated film star, reputedly a formidable consumer of Dry Martinis (and other spirituous beverages) – whose name, even if the story be correct, I would not dream of divulging – was addressing a large charity meeting in the Hollywood Bowl. Knowing that many of those present – from whom he hoped to raise substantial amounts – were fanatically teetotal, he thought he had best pay tribute to them. He said, in effect:

I know there are in this audience many who have never touched demon alcohol, nor did their fathers, nor will their children – and I want to say to you how much this abstinence has my respect. Yet this respect is tinged with sincere remorse for you – for when you wake up in the morning, that's as good as you're ever going to feel!

I feel the same way myself. So I thought it would be a nice gesture to dedicate this book to the Abstainers of the world, who will never read it, as a small recompense for what they are missing. We Dry Martinians are a generous-minded lot.

Ingredients

Aperitif by Kingsley Amis

I drank my first Dry Martini in a New York cocktail bar. This was surely as appropriate as losing one's virginity in Paris or, nearer yet, joining the Roman Catholic Church in Rome itself. Since that first one was quite soon followed by a second one and a third one, and possibly further ones, my memory of the occasion is imperfect, but I can still picture the bartender doing what I had thought was done only in the movies: pouring the gin and the vermouth into the shaker – yes, John, the shaker – *without looking*. And, of course, the drink was exactly the right size and perfectly blended.

America has given the world nothing finer or more cheering than this classic drink, not even jazz, which was born at the same time and flourished alongside it; it was *the* potable of the Jazz Age. But, now that that age is gone and jazz is dead, the Dry Martini is still alive and kicking as hard as ever. It's the only cocktail that is, outside certain specialized establishments, for the expense-account spender.

John Doxat has all the qualifications needed by a writer on drink: knowledge, experience (plenty of that), the practical approach, an eye for the revealing anecdote or out-of-the-way fact, spontaneous wit, and more. Who is better fitted to tackle the subject of this book than a man whose style is clear, dry, cool, flavoursome and balanced, all combining to produce a comfortable glow in the consumer?

Preface: The Purpose of the Mix

It was once reported that a gathering of wealthy women in California was holding a Dry Martini shindig when armed robbers invaded the house, intent on relieving them of jewels and cash. So profound was the martinian euphoria enjoyed by the celebrants that they ignored the menacing guns and cordially pressed the intruders to join them in a convivial glass. Entirely puzzled by this Martini-induced feminine insouciance, so different to the reaction customarily displayed by their victims, the gangsters withdrew with muttered apologies. The ladies continued their drinking undisturbed.

Such is one effect of the Dry Martini, though I must add that another may be that of the wife who complained that when viewing all-in wrestling on TV, whilst imbibing Martinis, it appeared to her that the men in the ring were wearing snap-brim hats.

The Martini spectrum is wide.

The magic of 'Dry Martini Time' was never better summarized than by the American essayist, Bernard de Voto, who was devoted to the cocktail and who before his lamented death contributed much sound drinking sense to the columns of *Harper's Magazine*.

Of that crepuscular period of détente, to which the French gave the poetic name *l'heure bleue*, when the Dry Martini is at its very best, he wrote:

> This is the violet hour, the hour of hush and wonder, where the affections glow again and valour is re-born, when the shadows deepen magically along the edge of the forest and

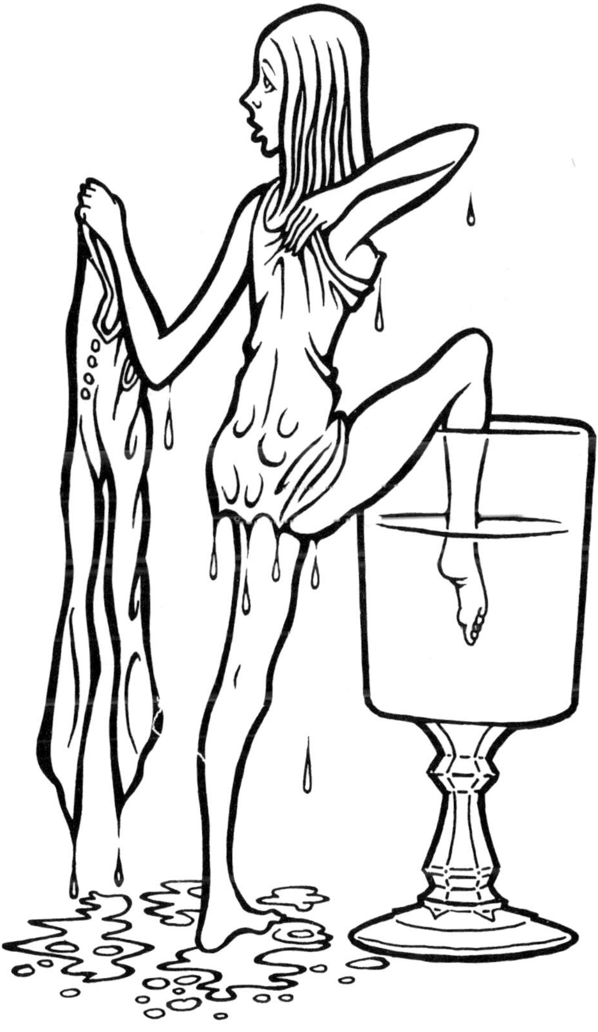

'I must get out of these wet clothes and into a Dry Martini'.

we believe that, if we watch carefully, at any moment we may see the unicorn.

Believe me, after occasional injudicious indulgence in Martinis, I *have* seen unicorns!

I append a facetious note to de Voto's prose elegy because, though the specific gravity of my subject is high, its levity is inherent. It has significant aspects, yet essentially the Dry Martini is a fun thing. This continually breaks through in the considerable space that influential writers have given it. My purpose is to collate and distil their wisdom and opinions and mix them with the fruits of my own researches, adding a garnish of comment, advice, folk-lore and joke-lore from numerous sources.

Thus, this is perhaps less a cocktail book than a cocktail of a book.

But enough of preface.

There is a much quoted saying of Alexander Woollcott – though some attribute it to other members of New York's once-celebrated literary coterie, the Algonquin Hotel's Round Table, whose loosely defined members were not sometimes above pinching each other's witticisms. I will parody Woollcott's epigram:

'I must get out of these wet words and into the Dry Martini.'

1. Personal History

For several years I nurtured the notion of consecrating a book to a sole alcoholic concoction – certainly the most celebrated mixed drink in the civilized world. Known, perhaps, to as many people who have never – or rarely – drunk it, as to those who have become its devotees. The Dry Martini is as much talked about, joked about, lauded, abused, as it is actually imbibed. Why this should be remains, and will remain, a mystery, for much concerning the Dry Martini is mysterious, verging on the mystical. Minutiae of its preparation will engender deep discussion amongst persons of high intellect. Escapism? In the field of *haute mixologisme* the world over, top professional bartenders will dispute tiny details of proportions of ingredients and mixing methods. No other mixed drink evokes a fraction of this interest. How can such a weird thing, that even escapes precise definition, have engendered such curiosity? Certainly the subject may be dismissed as trivial – so why do many serious people take it seriously? I do not pretend to answer these imponderables, but happily I have been placed in the position of being able to research, in greater depth than ever before, the origins, development, mutations and amusement to be found in this peculiar social phenomenon.

Let's start with a little personal history. It will set the book's tone.

I can only guess when I drank my first Dry Martini. It was quite likely to have been in March 1934, when, as a very young cub reporter in London for the *Yorkshire Post*, I attended a particularly swish press lunch at old Romano's in the Strand. Cocktails *ad lib* preceded a Lucullan repast at which rare wines were served. These were succeeded by vintage port and, so far as I was concerned, by indutiably my first memorable Hangover.

In my late teens, after I fled, in 1933, the dull luxury of family life for the comfortable freedom of journalism, I was omnibibulous – except for beer, which I detested until forced into accepting its merits by wartime shortage of classier potables.

As a cinema-goer, devoted to the point of mania, I easily adopted fashions from the screen – such as affecting a black snap-brim hat which I considered *de rigeur* for a newspaper-man, and which my father thought outrageously vulgar. Following repeal of Prohibition in the U.S., movies showed a good deal of smart social cocktail drinking – as opposed to previous rakish speakeasy boozing – and, though conjectural, I reckon it likely I first thus vicariously came into contact with the Dry Martini, epitome of sophistication. As a naïve adolescent, I grotesquely valued sophistication. Michael Parkinson's later experience exactly reflects my attitude.

Writing of the early influence the movies had on him in his formative years, in the *Spectator* of 23 November 1974, he said he thought '. . . I knew how to order a dry martini long before I needed the information.' He went on to describe how he experimented with this second-hand knowledge at the opening of a cocktail bar in Barnsley. This, he admitted, was an improbable innovation. '. . . it was not exactly a raging success and closed almost as soon as it opened. But not before it had claimed one victim: me.'

Intent on impressing his companion – 'she was, I recall, Miss Stocking Factory of 1963' – after ordering her preferred tipple of Port-and-Lemon, for himself he called for 'Vodka martini, rocks, lemon twist, no olive.' The bartender expressed good Yorkshire imcomprehension.

Dry Martinian

I repeated the order, loudly this time because I had the attention of the bar. He looked at me for a minute, then turned his back, and busied himself with the order. Miss Stocking Factory was looking at me with enraptured eyes, the rest of the clients quite obviously envied my man of the world panache. The barman turned from his endeavours and presented me with his version of a vodka martini. It was dark brown in colour, had a head on it like a good stout and was served in a pint pot. Moreover, it had half a dozen cherries floating in its foam.

It was the supreme invention of one man who had never heard of a vodka martini to another who knew how to say it but didn't know what it looked like . . .

There are, in different aspects of everyone's life, certain people or occasions that exercise critical influence. My career as a Dry Martinian might never have begun had I not come into the orbit of Perico Claude Jnr, of Valparaiso de Chile, whose sole memorial may be these few paragraphs: it is not a memorial he would have disdained.

Though it is only forty years ago, the era of which I now write seems scarcely less remote than the Regency – with which, indeed, it had some affinity. The Claudes were colossally wealthy: I do not use the adjective loosely. Highly literate, multi-lingual, talented in the tradition of Victorian dilettantism – and for most of the time supremely bored – Perico was for me the summation of plutocratic sophistication. Be it of insufficient duration to spoil, association with such rare social levels is immensely educative. But for Perico initiating me into the world of the Dorchester, the Paris Ritz, Vichy in its last days of high fashion, it might have been years later before I discovered the delights of vintage champagne, châteaux-bottled clarets, caviar blinys and Dry Martinis.

Perico was devoted to Dry Martinis: they stimulated an appetite jaded by excess of rich viands. When giving a party in his two-bedroom Dorchester suite – one room was used as a store for his luggage which he declined to entrust to the management's care – he would buy from

Asprey's, Bond Street, whatever was latest in Martini mixing gadgets, cocktail glasses and so on, disdaining the hotel's own splendid equipment. He would allow the hotel to provide the ingredients, but mixed the drinks himself, and his idea of ordering gin was to call for one bottle for every guest invited. I learned a lot about Dry Martinis – their virtues and defects – from Perico.

By 1938 I was an addicted Dry Martinian. For much of that year I was living in Paris, in a delightful flat near the Etoile. I acquired an evening drinking pattern that I don't recommend. For some months I frequented, in particular, a cocktail bar in rue Washington. I would order a goodly number of Dry Martinis to be set up simultaneously and in a row. I'd have a chat with the bartender, look at the drinks for a couple of minutes and then down them in quick succession. I can't recall where I acquired this ridiculous habit. The bartender mildly rebuked me – and quite rightly – and in due course I reverted to more sensible imbibition. If this looks as if I was living it up, I was. But these were the almost forgotten days of strong sterling and sagging franc: my beautifully furnished two-bedroom apartment cost me £2·50 a week inclusive of electricity and gas. Also, I had discovered that one could – again, how remote it seems – invest (no, gamble) on the Wall Street market without a penny of collateral. Blessed United Steel: how many Dry Martinis you unwittingly bought me!

It was around then that I found how important was the ambience in which one drank Dry Martinis. I did not particularly care for them in Harry's New York Bar (the famous 'Sank Roo Doe Noo') – though I ingested many other cocktails there – but they went perfectly in the Ritz and Crillon.

My gracious living did not abruptly stop in 1939. Early in 1940 I was engaged in as phoney a section of the phoney war as could be imagined. The War Office posted me to a non-existent appointment in France. When this was pointed out, they declined to admit their mistake, and, to

JD
GIN
VINO VERM
DOXY
SEND ICE
S.O.ICE

emphasize their omniscience, promoted me. So there I was, in Le Havre with nothing to do but enjoy the facilities of the opulent Hôtel Frascati – the Army's H.Q. – and the exceptional restaurants and bars of the city. The Dry Martinis were better in Rouen, whither I went when the unit to which I had been posted was eventually established: the bartender in the Hôtel de la Poste really knew his job. For an army man, our mess steward, in a neighbouring château, was pretty handy with the mixer. Many a pleasant pre-dinner session we had, chilled glass in hand, sitting on our terrace with panoramic views across the Seine. We were drinking cocktails there when a despatch-rider burst in – a most unseemly intrusion. However, disapproval gave way to dismay when he told the C.O. that he had just seen some Germans in a café a few miles away. No non-mobile H.Q. ever crossed a river faster than we did.

I didn't drink a Dry Martini for quite a long time after that. I had the basic ingredients all right when we were evacuated from La Rochelle, for I managed to get all our mess wines and spirits, of which I had charge, on board the collier in which we sailed a few days after the French capitulation – 5000 of us in a ship designed for a crew of fifty. I guarded – and issued to fellow officers – several cases of House of Lords Gin, vermouth, Scotch, wines. But, of course, no ice: there wasn't even enough water. Have you ever tried drinking gin and vermouth out of a tin mug in baking June sunshine with a liberal coating of coal dust on everything? Actually, it's not at all bad. What food we had went to the other ranks. After five days I arrived at Newport, starving but happy.

They tried hard in London during the war – but it's no use pretending Dry Martinis were up to much. Essentials were in very short supply. I'm afraid there was a good deal of cheating when the Americans arrived – lots of ice, a little ersatz vermouth, dip the rim of the glass in gin so it will taste strong. Not in the best places of course, but where you get G.I.s you get clip-joints. Best forget this period, the nadir of the Dry Martini.

After peace broke out, it wasn't immediately all joy. Vermouth supplies normalized much earlier than those of good gin. But there was soon a revived interest in cocktails and a good many competitions. Would the Dry Martini survive the years of drought, the introduction of new mixes? We know the answer was yes, and I attribute this largely to American influence. It was mainly to the U.S.A. that London-distilled gin had been diverted during the war and distillation there had not suffered the dramatic reduction it had in Britain. Drinking patterns had not received the knock they had in Europe. Americans began to pour across the Atlantic and what they wanted poured for them, on the great liners and in their hotel bars, was largely what they had drunk before Pearl Harbour – Scotch, cocktails, and particularly the king of cocktails, the Dry Martini.

Demobbed and back in journalism – albeit a different branch to my pre-war career – I found myself in the free-loading business. I wasn't being at all well paid so I was grateful to be able to drink as many Dry Martinis as I liked at the expense of some company whose P.R.O. thought I was worth cultivating. Not always Dry Martinis – but frequently Dry Martinis.

In 1962, having a wife and two thirsts to support, I was supremely fortunate in being asked to join London's senior gin distillers – and subsequently was given additional responsibilities in connection with other important spirits. This reformed and civilized my drinking habits and I started to learn about drink instead of merely pouring it down. I became fascinated by the social history of drinking. In 1966 my researches into cocktails impelled me to write my first book. A principal chapter concerned the Dry Martini, though I followed popular error when it came to describing its origin. I was able to correct this in my second, and more voluminous publication, and from that dated my idea that the Dry Martini deserved a book to itself.

I believe I finally decided to write it during a lunch in

Stone's Chophouse. My guest was that most versatile of writers – and considerable authority on potables – Kingsley Amis. We had just toured Booth's Red Lion Distillery in Clerkenwell – London's historic distilling centre – and I was enlarging Kingsley's ginformation. Knowing we shared a love of Dry Martinis, on our way to the restaurant I explained that as a matter of self-discipline I only drink Martinis on Fridays. It was a Wednesday. We ensconced ourselves in the upstairs bar, whose presiding *maître des cocktails* is Peter Dorelli. He holds my personal trophy – it took him three years to win it – for producing the '99·9% Perfect High & Dry Martini'.

A waiter approached to take our order.

'What day of the week is it?' I asked.

'Wednesday, sir.'

'I think it's Friday.'

'With respect, sir, it's Wednesday.'

'Please ask Peter,' I said.

The young waiter, who knew me and whose Savoy Group training prevented from indicating any suggestion I had gone dotty, went to the bar for consultation. He returned.

'I am sorry, sir, you are right. It's Friday.'

'Then we'll have two Specials' – my local description for mammoth Dry Martinis.

Kingsley expressed interest in this substitution of days. We went in to lunch, rather late. I promised Kingsley some literature and extra notes on a point or two he had raised, which I despatched that afternoon. I was a trifle surprised he sent no acknowledgement, for he had struck me as possessing an almost old-world courtesy. However, ten days later I got a postcard from Brighton thanking me for my hospitality and information. In a sentence he explained the delay. 'Unfortunately,' he wrote, 'last week I declared four Fridays.'

2. Of Alcohol and Cocktails

The Dry Martini is the King of Cocktails. I realize that statement is provocative: I stand by it. It is also the most powerful of all sensible mixed drinks. Thus, we had better deal with the dual subjects of alcohol and cocktails in general.

I am quite aware of the dangers of alcohol. I assume that people intelligent enough to appreciate this book are also cognisant of them. I prefer to consider alcohol's virtues, as did the great authority, Dr Maurice E. Chafetz, as head of the alcohol clinic at Massachusetts General Hospital, Boston, who, in his *Liquor – the Servant of Man*, summed up his immense knowledge: 'Good liquor and good drinking experience are the best possible tonics. It relaxes you, it heightens pleasure, and makes you feel good . . .' I feel that exactly sets out the merits of the Dry Martini. A notable English expert, a psychiatrist and physician, cutting through the verbiage of a seminar on alcohol, stated his firm opinion that alcohol is the 'cheapest and safest of all tranquilizers'. Before the war, a friend of mine who was to achieve eminence with *The Times*, finding himself under strain, consulted that celebrated diagnostician and Royal physician, Lord Dawson of Penn. He recommended nothing more than that his patient sit down with a cocktail or two before dinner. It worked. In much more modern times, my personal assistant – without whose ethical coercion this book would never have been completed – was taking anti-depressant pills. (I can't think why, since working with me is essentially stimulating!) They did not work – in fact made her feel ill. Taking a second opinion, a wiser doctor said, 'Throw away those pills and have a decent tot of good alcohol.' No more trouble.

But like all alcohol, Dry Martinis must not be abused. To toss down several in quick succession is not only uncivilized and an insult to a great drink; it is to court insobriety and kill appetite. This sort of uncouth drinking was characterized by the famous New York restaurateur, Toots Shor, speaking to columnist Bob Considine: 'A guy comes in here and he looks like he's fresh from taking lessons as an altar-boy. He has one Martini and he wants to clean out the joint. A loving couple comes in: you never saw such a happy couple. Then the guy or the dame drinks a Martini and you've got to get the waiter to separate them.' Toots then drank a Martini.

Whilst I put into circulation the phrase, 'There's no such thing as one Dry Martini', I believe the Martini must be treated with respect, bordering on reverence. Prepared with brisk care, it should be ingested decorously and at sensible speed, sipped and savoured. This will induce desire for another. Then it will perform the gentle miracle described by Dr Chafetz: it will soothe nervous tension, brighten conversation, sharpen the appetite and cast a benign aura over any occasion, so that part of the most ordinary day acquires a special gloss. Other cocktails have their place and purpose: none has quite achieved the social grace nor earned the eminence of the Dry Martini.

What is a cocktail? Strangely, it has never been legally defined (if one omits certain special cases involving bottled cocktails and proprietary spirits). An endeavour to do so was made by Kiamram Halil in the *New Law Journal* of 20 February 1973:

A mixture of spirituous liquor(s), in equal or unequal proportions, to which non-alcoholic beverages, fruit juices, bitters, and sugar may sometimes be added depending upon the individual requirements of recipes (which may also specify the addition of egg whites or yolks, cocktail onions, olives or fruit peel) and shaken in a cocktail shaker or stirred in a mixing glass with ice cubes, intact, cracked or crushed, as the case may be, providing that the strength of the said mixture does not fall below 28° proof spirit.

That's quite a good effort. Another, equally unofficial, notion is that a cocktail is a mixture of three or more ingredients; but does ice count as an ingredient? (Does a cocktail even have to be alcoholic – what I have named 'mocktail'?) The question is not wholly academic, at least so far as Britain is concerned: whisky, gin, rum and vodka are required to be served in measures of not less than one-sixth of a gill and a notice of the minimum measure used must be displayed. (Brandy, through a bureaucratic oversight, was omitted.) It is generally understood – though the matter has not been tested in court – that a cocktail need not conform to the rule about minimum measures. Thus, a definition of what constitutes a cocktail has potential importance, becoming what lawyers call 'a nice point'.

So the cocktail remains legally nebulous, though in social usage well understood. Nebulous, too, is the origin of the odd word. I know at least nine theories, mainly fanciful. Of the tenable ideas I prefer the derivation apparently propounded by Dr Samuel Johnson in my Interlude 'Boswell on Booze'. It is logical that a hard-drinking horsey fraternity, given to imbibing sundry 'mixed' drinks, would to some potions have attached the word 'cocktail'. You may like one of the romantic legends, but I'll stick to a more probable premise. The first description of a cocktail as recognizable to us was in an American journal, *The Balance*, in 1806: 'A stimulating liquor composed of spirits of any sort, sugar, water [ice] and bitters.' The Americans were always more interested in mixed drinks than anyone else and more adventurous. With the exception of Collins, I can think of no famous cocktail – including, of course, the Dry Martini – that was not American invented: though not always in the U.S.A. In earlier times cocktails were taken to outdoor sporting or

social occasions: their use as aperitifs is of much later origin. In Britain, early mentions of cocktails occur in *Tom Brown's Schooldays*, naturally in connection with that prototype bounder, Flashman; and in *Martin Chuzzlewit*. Cocktails did not for a long time achieve social acceptance in Britain. When Galsworthy wished further to emphasize what a cad Monty Dartie was – in *The Forsyte Saga* – he had him drink a cocktail during Queen Victoria's funeral procession.

The first cocktail book inevitably was American; in 1862 *The Bon Vivant's Guide or How To Mix Drinks* was published by Jerry Thomas, a Californian who gained fame in The Metropolitan Hotel, New York City. He toured Europe with a well-publicized £1000-worth of silver mixing equipment and certainly must have done much to advance interest in cocktails in the right circles. It was Jerry Thomas who evolved the 'Martinez' cocktail which has given rise to a totally incorrect supposition regarding the birth of the Dry Martini. More anon about that.

By the turn of the century, in most capitals the Smart Set were drinking cocktails, but nothing like to the extent Americans were: the first American (i.e. cocktail) bar was not opened in London until 1910. Prohibition was what really put cocktails on the map. Legally deprived of good alcohol, with inferior hooch Americans exerted their natural talent for mixed drinks in order to disguise the abominable taste by exotic supplementations. Those rich enough and fortunate enough to buy good bootlegged spirits equally took to dreaming up esoteric, often horrendous, mixes, and the habit spread overseas, giving birth to the absurdities of the Cocktail Age, *c.* 1922–36. Trend-setters like Somerset Maugham and leading lights of stage, and Society with a big S – or their progeny, the Bright Young Things – were seen to partake of a profusion of cocktails. Not all the older generation by any means approved. The first serving of a cocktail in a play, *Spring Cleaning* (1925), by the highly fashionable playwright, Frederick Lonsdale, helped set a seal of approval. The ascendant Noël Coward quickly followed by serving four cocktails in his sensation-provoking *The Vortex*. Amidst the proliferation of cocktails, established favourites continued to dominate, and comfortably survived the collapse of the Cocktail Age as the world took on more sombre tones.

Survivor supreme has been the Dry Martini.

Historical note on spirit

The separation of pure alcohol from the rest of an alcoholic liquid was practised centuries ago: precisely how many, none knows. Claims are made that the Chinese practised distillation before the Christian era. That alcohol vaporizes at a lower temperature than water was known to ancient Moorish savants, though they probably used the resultant spirit as a base for perfumes. We owe the word alcohol to the Arabic *Al'koh'l* (kohl), a very refined metallic cosmetic powder: to distil is a form of refining.

In the west, spirit was known and valued by the eleventh century. It was certainly distilled from wine and that it was known as *aqua vitae* (water of life) emphasizes its medicinal use. By the fourteenth century distilling was reasonably well established in France and Germanic lands and detailed instructions for distilling were published in 1358. Rather over a century later, a publication in Augsburg indicates that *eau de vie*, a crude brandy, was being employed socially, confirmed by a Nuremburg decree of 1496 forbidding sale of spirits on Sundays and saints' days. Distilling apparatus was illustrated in a book published in 1526 and one dated 1532 shows equipment of some complexity and the rudiments of rectification – secondary distillation to remove impurities from the rough, weakish spirits (low wines) which are the usual product of first distillation.

The use of spirits was slow to come to England (though popular much earlier in Ireland and then Scotland): *aqua vitae* was barely known until the sixteenth century and English distilling hardly existed. Publication in 1525 of an English translation of a German work, under the title *The Virtuose Boke of Distullacyon of the Waters of all Manner of Herbs* must have provided some impetus. But not until the introduction of gin, and its encouragement, as we shall see, did the English really take to spirits. The Distillers livery company of the City of London had been granted a charter by Charles I. It was founded by the remarkable Sir Theodore de Mayerne-Turquet – born in Geneva the year Europe's oldest extant commercial distillers was established – who was physician to one French and three English monarchs. Under his authority, the Distillers published a book, which quotes rules forbidding the sale of 'low wines' and giving a large number of recipes for spirituous herbal concoctions – there is no mention of juniper (gin) – which significantly were wholly medicinal. At this time the English upper classes were drinking some imported *eau de vie*, to which they gave the name Brandywine – a corruption of the Dutch for 'burnt (distilled) wine'. But the masses scarcely knew spirits unless it be a sailor's acquaintance with rum or the soldiers' occasional campaign contact with distillates of the Low Countries, to the imbibing of which before battle we owe the phrase 'Dutch courage'.

The Spanish introduced distilling to the New World, sugar cane providing the base for admirable spirit. They quickly established vineyards in California, and surely distilled some of the wine. But the first mention of distilling in North America does not occur until 1640, in New Amsterdam (New York); the Dutch would not want to go without their gin. Yet certainly some colonists from Britain – particularly Irish and Scots – would not have been slow to try to copy the spirits of their homelands. Only two years after the foundation of the United States, the new republic endeavoured to tax spirits, the production of which was extremely widespread. Initially, this was about as successful as Prohibition.

This is all a long way, in time, quality and taste, from the fine spirits of today, but as we savour our Dry Martini it is worth reflecting on what made it all possible.

3. The Beginnings - before and after Signor Martini

New York City: a pleasant day in 1910, and into the cocktail bar of the Knickerbocker Hotel came sprightly seventy-year-old John D. Rockefeller, prototype oil titan. 'Good evening, sir,' said Martini di Arma di Taggia, the head bartender. 'I have something special for you.'

'Not my usual gin-and-French?'

'Just a little different, Mr Rockefeller.'

Signor Martini poured some imported London Dry Gin into a bar glass – I use the old-fashioned description – added ice, as much dry vermouth as he had of gin, and a dash of orange bitters. He stirred the mix and poured it into a shallow glass, squeezed a sliver of lemon rind over the drink and placed in it a green olive impaled on a cocktail stick.

'Well, that does look a little different,' said John D.

He sipped it.

'Very pleasing,' he said. 'We'll have to call it Martini's cocktail.' He sipped again. 'No, the *Dry* Martini!' John D. finished the drink, tipped 25 cents – his later reputation as a tightwad was a legend he enjoyed – and proceeded to whatever business rendezvous he had, whence doubtless he would emerge potentially a few million dollars the richer. He still had twenty-seven years of life ahead: to what age he drank is not recorded.

That is a fictional reconstruction of the origination of the Dry Martini. But I believe it is a personalized dramatization of *fact*, which I published for the first time in my

Drinks and Drinking (Ward Lock, London, 1972), an encyclopaedia of limited distribution. The information came via my old friend, Mr James Porter. A much travelled senior executive in the international oil business, Jim Porter was a wartime colleague of mine and drinking companion in the arid depths of Yorkshire in 1942: no Martinis there! In the early seventies he recorded an interview at the Savoia Majestic Hotel, Genoa, with the celebrated Luigi, then acting as what one might describe as heap bartender ex-officio: he subsequently retired, and further communication with him proved impracticable due to his advanced age.

Luigi was known as something of a romancer, yet on this particular point his reminiscences are so factual, vivid and logical, that until anyone produces better evidence – and I'll be very surprised if they do – I put forward Signor Martini as the sole begetter of the cocktail that bears his name.

To return to Luigi. He emigrated to the U.S.A. in 1912, and was lucky to get there. He intended working his way in the *Titanic* but failed at the last moment to get a berth. Arriving in New York, he naturally turned to the big Italian community and found a job as a very junior assistant in the bar of the Knickerbocker. He progressed quickly and was soon working with Signor Martini: he learned the mysteries of Martini-mixing from the original maestro himself. Martini returned to his native Italy, and Genoa eventually became his final resting place. Like as not, he worked for a time in the Roaring Twenties – height of the Cocktail Age – at the very smart resort of San Remo, where Dry Martinis were being made with the first important Italian *dry* vermouth: coincidentally, it bore his name, Martini. But the Dry Martini was named for the man, not the brand of vermouth. Initially, dry vermouth came exclusively from France: only in our time has internationally-produced Martini Extra Dry become universally favoured by Dry Martinians.

I feel sure Luigi was recalling the truth about Rockefeller

'Will you never learn, Cecil, the green one for DRY Martini'.

liking a Dry Martini, for which the Knickerbocker soon became renowned. Not that everyone liked them. Luigi also remembered that Caruso, an habitué of the bar, could not be persuaded from champagne. When the Dry Martini was first copied by other bars I have no idea, but I doubt if it took long. At least competitors and copyists gave credit where it was due: this transmogrification of a simple iced gin and French into a subtle cocktail was known from the start as a Dry Martini. The alchemy of mixing separately, the hint of bitters, the touch of lemon peel, opened a new chapter in the history of mixed drinks.

We had best dispose of the fallacious claim that the great Jerry Thomas, whom I have previously lauded for his pioneer contributions to mixology, invented the Dry Martini. He did indeed evolve a *Martinez* cocktail – subsequently corrupted to 'Martini' by some writers. In his Californian, pre-Metropolitan days, Jerry concocted a special drink for a traveller and so liked it himself that he recalled the ingredients, and subsequently published the recipe, and, unable to remember more about his customer than that he was proceeding to a township called Martinez, so titled the mix. It consisted of a dash of bitters (type unspecified), two dashes of maraschino, an ounce of sweet Old Tom gin, a wine glass of vermouth – inevitably sweet – and two small lumps of ice. This would have been a cocktail sugary to the point of sickliness. It conforms to popular mixed American drinks of the mid-to-late nineteenth century. It was doubtless stimulating – not to say nourishing – for a weary traveller. But it bears no resemblance to a Dry Martini.

In this I am sorry to have to contradict Jamie Maxtone Graham who, in an otherwise faultless article in *Gourmet* Magazine in 1968, perpetrated the Jerry Thomas heresy. I am indebted to *Gourmet* – supreme vade-mecum of

Martinimiser

cosmopolitan *bon vivants* – and to its editor, Arthur W. Miller, for many kindnesses in connection with this book. He sent me the issue containing Jamie's feature: I had mislaid mine. I helped in its preparation and was flattered by its reference to me as '. . . John Doxat, foremost among London's thinking drinkers.' (I wouldn't mind that as an epitaph.)

That the Dry Martini did not exist in Jerry Thomas's day, nor until the current century, is further evidenced by an important book on mixed drinks; New York, 1882 – by Harry Johnson, self-styled Publisher and Bartender. This was in print in 1900, if not later, for I have an edition of that year. It takes a mild knock at *The Bon Vivants Guide* for Johnson's title was *The New and Improved Illustrated Bartenders' Manual or How To Mix Drinks of the present style*. That is, not the old style, e.g. Thomas's. Johnson includes the Blue Blazer, which Thomas invented at the Metropolitan; and when it comes to 'Martini Cocktail' the *Bartenders' Manual* has a variation of the Thomas recipe:

(use a large bar glass) [we'd call that a mixing-glass]
Fill the glass up with ice;
2 or 3 dashes of gum [gomme] syrup (be careful in not using too much)
2 or 3 dashes of bitters (Boker's genuine only); [who was Boker?]
1 dash curaçao or absinthe, if required; [not too didactic, was Johnson]
½ wine glass of Old Tom gin;
½ wine glass of vermouth.
Stir up well with a spoon; strain into a fancy cocktail glass; put in a cherry or a medium-sized olive, if required; add a squeeze of a piece of lemon peel on the top, and serve.

Again, a sweetish cocktail though probably drier than Thomas's. There is a line engraving illustrating this drink (copyright 1888) – it shows two versions; one in something very like a modern Martini glass (if there be such an object) and one in a tumbler with cracked ice – 'on the rocks' as we would say, though textually Johnson makes no allusion to thus serving what the picture captions as 'Martine' cocktail. Possibly this is a misprint, though it occurs to me that the name (again that corruption of Martinez?) may not have then been finalized. It needed Signor Martini to resolve that.

I quote this recipe to show emphatically that the *Dry* Martini was yet to come. That the illustration is dated six years after the book's first edition – the second and revised edition came out in 1888 – indicates that only after he had written his book did Johnson recognize Martinez/Martine/Martini cocktail. Whilst inarguably Johnson did not concoct a Dry Martini, he was moving that way – at least in the preparation, and in the employment of lemon rind and optional olive. The illustrations show no olive (or cherry) in the cocktail, nor lemon peel.

Harry Johnson has got lost in mixing history, and I think his obvious contemporary importance deserves resuscitation. He was a Californian, like the better remembered Jerry Thomas, whom it is likely he knew. He learned his craft in San Francisco, leaving there in 1868 to open a saloon in Chicago which he described (he did not share the modesty becoming to a professional bartender) as 'what was generally recognized to be the largest and finest establishment of the kind in this country'. This place was burned out in the 1871 great fire of Chicago. Ruined, Johnson got employment in Boston, but soon went on to New York City where he 'was employed in one of the well-known hostelries of the Metropolis until enabled to begin a business of my own, which has since been pre-eminently successful'.

It appears that during his Californian days, he had published a *Bartenders' Manual* – forerunner of his later book – which he claims was the first of its type in the U.S.A., and thus in the world. It sold 10,000 copies. Did this publication – I would dearly like to see it – precede Jerry Thomas's work? Was *it* the first ever cocktail book? And was the first cocktail competition that held in 1869 when Johnson was challenged by 'five of the most popular and scientific bartenders of the day (including Thomas?) to engage in a tourney of skill, at New Orleans, with the consequence that to me was awarded the championship of the United States'?

Harry Johnson's career ended just when the Dry Martini came on the scene. I don't know when he retired or died, and I hope that this book may fall into the hands of savants of bibulosity with the knowledge to enlighten me on such details – and others. For instance, there must be persons alive who drank a Dry Martini made by its inventor.

His first Dry Martinis differed only in detail from those we ingest today. Not until after World War I did the proportions of equal amounts of dry gin and vermouth start to vary in favour of a higher percentage of spirit. In my early Martini days, the rule was about one-third vermouth to two-thirds gin. Orange bitters were usually added, the lemon peel was customarily not dropped into the drink and an olive was virtually taken for granted. Local practice varied of course. Earlier, more powerful Martinis were being drunk by such well lubricated celebrities as Hemingway and Fitzgerald in Paris: Hemingway later became addicted to Daiquiris and lost the Dry Martini habit. I don't imagine W. C. Fields had much vermouth in his constant companion, a vacuum flask of Dry Martini. I remember 'specially strong ones being made in Harry's New York Bar in the French capital, though, as I have said, I did not feel its hectic boozing atmosphere was quite right for the cocktail. (It was more suited to the Sidecar and White Lady, said to have been invented there, or plain Scotch.)

It was really only in the later 1940s that Martinis started getting drier and drier, in defiance of many pundits who deplored what they saw as a vulgarization of the most delicate and sophisticated of mixes. Nor was the reputation of the Dry Martini exactly enhanced by constant resource to it by the dipsomaniac superbly played by Ray Milland in that horrifyingly brilliant piece of cinematic propaganda for Alcoholics Anonymous, *The Lost Weekend.* How many now remember that film? Martini-drinkers are made of sterner stuff than its self-indulgent anti-hero.

By the sixties the very dry Dry Martini was fairly common; it is now almost universal. Where do we go from here? A return to what many might consider a more cultured mix? More mutations? There's no crystal ball in the bottom of my Martini glass.

Mixing Glass

4. Tools of the Craft

Elsewhere I deal at some length with the making of Dry Martinis, the assumption there being that ideal equipment is to hand. Principally, this section is for novices in the Dry Martinian mystique.

In fact, the drink does not require any special equipment at all. Providing you have the proper ingredients to hand, you can make a superb Martini in any old jug, stir with a fork, strain it with a kitchen spoon and serve it in a sherry glass. (That is why I don't mention equipment in my chapters on 'The Essentials'.) But I bet you are not going to be so uncouth. This élite mix encourages glamour; glamour informed by good taste. The aesthetics of Dry Martiniana are not to be denied.

There are Martini mixing jugs. These have the advantage of a handle for ease of pouring. Some have a pinched lip that theoretically prevents ice from getting into the glass: in practice, annoying small fragments tend to escape. Unless you are serving 'on the rocks', you don't want ice except in the mixing vessel. Other jugs have built-in metal strainers – quite effective but not always removable for cleaning. Nor are jugs truly professional; bartenders never employ them. Most Dry Martinians wish to emulate top professional methods.

So we come to the most usual and traditional container, a mixing glass, pedantically a bar glass. I think this should be fairly solid and unornamented, and the width of the top should be just right to take a spring-rimmed strainer (usually a 'Hawthorn'). This type can be taken apart for washing: absolute cleanliness of equipment is vital. Hence, whilst I have seen some very attractive silver-rimmed mixing glasses, I cannot fully approve of them: some metal polish might adhere. I suppose an untarnishable solid gold rim would be fine: I've never seen one but they certainly exist (try Tiffany's or Asprey's?). My special mixing glass comes from the latter emporium's lovely Bond Street establishment. It is straight-sided, fairly thick, plain, and unusually tall – 14 inches. It holds around two pints, and has an 18-inch glass mixing-rod. It's wonderful for building gigantic party Dry Martinis, but for day-to-day use I employ a utilitarian professional glass, and a stout silver-plated bar spoon of conventional size.

A useful adjunct is a very sharp knife, preferably non-staining, for shaving off those important zests of lemon peel.

I emphasize plain mixing glasses, but I do have a cut-glass one – rarely used: I like to see the ice. There is no objection to more elaborately decorated ones provided they are not coloured nor of vulgar design. Engraved glasses may be extremely attractive but deep engraving encourages fragility. And I must come down heavily against mixing glasses with fancy measurement scales on them or written recipes – use those for ordinary cocktails if you must, but not for a Dry Martini or you risk social ostracism in the upper echelons of mixology.

Good taste must also inform your attitude to the glasses in which you serve your Dry Martinis. A prime consideration is that they be of sufficient size so that a nobly proportioned Dry Martini may be strained into them without the glass being filled: a decent freeboard is not only advisable to minimize spillage but a brimful glass doesn't look good. The glasses must be sufficiently robust to endure refrigeration and must, of course, have stems so they may be held without warm hands touching the bowl. Not only is it undesirable to reduce the cocktail's frigidity but one doesn't wish to court frostbite by prolonged contact with an icy surface: possible origin of the phrase 'Ma teeny hand is frozen', attributed to a black New Orleans bartender when making too many Dry Martinis in quick succession.

I do feel that Dry Martinis should not be served in glasses that are in any way over-decorative; let this nectar speak for itself; let the surface be so smooth and the glass so crystal clear that the magical frosting lends enchantment. You cannot achieve this with heavily cut or ornamental vessels. No odd shapes please, and not too shallow a glass – for a veteran Dry Martinian's hands may not be the world's steadiest. Within the bounds of commonsense, the glass employed is a matter for personal choice. For my money, it's a fine, plain wine goblet of five to eight ounces' capacity.

Exaggerated onion or olive sticks are to be avoided. Again expressing a personal opinion, I opt for the plainest wooden sticks which cannot taint the cocktail, and are disposable: a Dry Martini deserves more than an ornate plastic pin.

We have now covered the basic tools of the craft. You may wish to complement your mixing glass with an ice bucket of appropriate quality, and many accessories are available such as electric ice crushers for 'on the rocks' Martinis. But the keynote of Dry Martini equipment is a refined simplicity.

5. The Essentials

Whilst that notable American Dry Martini fancier Bernard de Voto said that 'Sound practice begins with ice . . .' – and whilst I consider ice extremely important – it is gin and vermouth with which we must firstly be concerned. Frederick Birmingham in *The Esquire Drink Book* put it perfectly when he wrote: 'A Martini to be worthy of the name must be made with the very finest Vermouth and positively sublime Gin. Otherwise, it is a sell and a swindle and incompetent to set the mood for a meal.'

The notion that as it is an iced cocktail, a Dry Martini can be made with cheap, weak (what is sometimes known in Britain as 'cocktail') gin and any dry vermouth could not be more erroneous and if you are going to use second-rate ingredients you might as well spare your time and save your palate. Both in private homes – and, I regret to admit, in some bars – I have had alleged Dry Martinis that were a disgrace to the title. It was always the inferiority of the gin or vermouth that was to blame, abetted by sloppy mixing. The Dry Martini is one drink you had better forget if you want to economize: quality is the keynote. Top professional bartenders know that and they can recognize a proper Dry Martinian by the way he orders. But I won't say that everyone, always, every time gets the same treatment!

As to Gin, it must be remembered that, on its own, the description 'London Dry Gin' has little significance: in numerous countries, appalling spirit is quite legally sold bearing the words. Only in a few countries is London held to describe the place of production: in most, including Britain and the U.S.A., it is broadly indicative of a style of gin – 'London Dry' as opposed to, say, Dutch (Geneva). Whilst it can be argued that the very best dry gin comes from London itself, it is a fact that in the U.S.A., Canada, Europe, South Africa, Australia, New Zealand – and many other places – dry gin is produced under the auspices of a handful of famous London distillers to exactly the same standards of quality as that which they distil in – and export from – the English capital. The best of these local distillations can satisfy the most particular Dry Martinian. For perfectionists there is a tiny list of celebrated dry gins only distilled in London. The reputation of the London distiller whose name is on the bottle is the drinker's sole guarantee.

Though used in smaller quantity, vermouth is as essential to a Dry Martini as the gin: a poor dry vermouth will wreck a cocktail made with the finest London dry gin. There are very few high quality extra dry vermouths. Again, like gin, these are produced in many countries but always under names that are household words. With both gin and vermouth 'name dropping' is not a snobbish prerogative: it is a necessity.

Both these products deserve an historical outline, which I append. In each instance I have added brief production notes, which may be skipped by those who believe such technicalities to be a frivolous intrusion in a serious volume.

However, before we pass on to gin and vermouth, let us consider a few other ingredients of the classic cocktail. To return to Mr de Voto: one of his correspondents completed the recipe for his notion of the perfect Dry Martini with '. . . and five hundred pounds of ice!' Watery ice, dirty ice, ice made with unsatisfactory water – these can ruin the best ingredients. Ideally, one wants *hard* ice, which really means good commercial ice that comes in big blocks and can be broken into lumps of required size. Such ice is quick-frozen which is why it is 'hard', albeit that it may not invariably be the purest. It does not melt as quickly as ice from a domestic refrigerator, which has

frozen more slowly and is 'soft'. A plastic bag, or container, part filled with pure water and frozen in a deep-freezer is more satisfactory. Ice from machines that turn out little roundels or cubes varies in hardness according to its speed of refrigeration. Ice is easily contaminated by proximity to unwanted flavours, especially fish.

A traditional ingredient of a classic Dry Martini, listed in most not-too-modern recipe books, is orange bitters, but these are increasingly rarely used. Orange bitters are traditionally made by macerating a special type of bitter orange in a mild pure spirit: a little sugar is added. Today concentrated essence of orange is usually employed – just as effectively.

If you are an olive character, use high quality green ones, not the black variety – and, of course, never stuffed ones. Pearl onions (for a Gibson) should be well drained from the vinegary fluid in which they are preserved. Lemons should be of a thick-skinned variety: it's the citric oil from the rind you require, no juice. Wash lemons to remove any preservative.

Ingredients for the wilder mutations to which I refer elsewhere are hardly worth considering. It's your gin and vermouth that are absolutely vital.

6. Blithe Spirit of the Dry Martini - Gin

'Eureka! Genever!' That is certainly *not* what Franciscus de la Boe exclaimed when he initially tasted what was to make possible the Dry Martini. The whole business is somewhat obscure: Franciscus seems also to have gone under the name Sylvius. All we know for certain is that an elixir compounded from oil of juniper and pure spirit was first distilled in mid-sixteenth century in the medical faculty of the University of Leyden. Though crude spirits were being drunk in everyday life in some parts of Europe, every famous distillation has had a medicinal origin. Franciscus (Sylvius) belonged to the type of alchemist-cum-pioneer physician in whose domain principally lay the craft of distilling, certainly of good distilling. Since juniper's virtues had been recognized long since, it appears a trifle odd that no-one had previously infused it into alcohol – though it had been mixed with wine. Perhaps they had, and Sylvius (Franciscus) simply perfected an earlier recipe. At all events, eventually only the distillate introduced to Scotland by Irish missionary-doctors was to rival the successor of Leyden's invention.

An interesting theory was propounded by Mr L. W. Marrison, that the word gin derives from the Italian for juniper, *ginevra*. Insofar as Italy produces much juniper, this is logical, but all other authorities agree that the progression was from the French for the herb, *genièvre*, to the Dutch *genever* (or *jenever*), corrupted to Geneva – probably

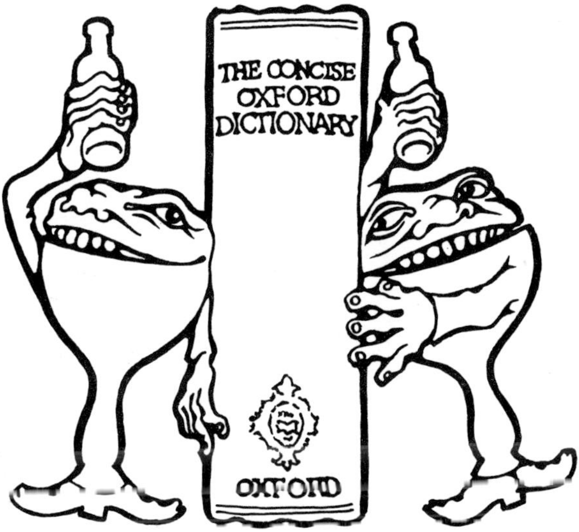

Ginerically speaking

by the English – and certainly by them shortened to gin. Though gin was being produced commercially at Schiedam in 1575, not for some time did it spread to Britain. It is to be surmised that soldiers, sailors and traders brought back the odd flagon of the new spirit, manifestly an improvement on earlier rough continental 'strong waters'. Yet there was only mild concern with it until the dramatic events of 1688, when James I was expelled and William of Orange came from the Netherlands to reign over England with his Stuart consort, Mary, as co-sovereign. Before then, in 1673, Parliament had received a petition from what today we would call the 'farmers' lobby' asking that, to protect the use of English grain for brewing (and distilling), the import of brandy, rum, tea and coffee be prohibited. The petition wrapped up its argument in specious theories that the health of the common people would benefit by these prohibitions. Nothing happened

Stirred – Not Shaken

'Strives the woodcock with the gin'
Shakespeare. The Third Part of Henry VI. *I. iv.*

immediately, for politics were in turmoil. But one of the first Acts of the new reign gave the farmers – which primarily meant the great land-owning aristocracy and gentry – their way. The Act declared its intention as being to encourage;

the distillation of brandy and spirits from corn. First, the trade and commerce of France [whither James had fled] being prohibited, and all their goods from being imported into this kingdom; and whereas good and wholesome Brandy, *aqua vitae* and spirits may be made from corn; for the encouragement therefore of the making of Brandy, strong waters and spirits from malted corn, and for the greater consumption of corn and the advantage of tillage in this kingdom, the King, Queen, and the Parliament assembled have thus ordained. . . .

This effectively granted every Englishman the right to distil spirits. It may be noted that brandy was not considered then necessarily to be a by-product of the grape. The Act opened a spirituous floodgate. At the beginning of the eighteenth century, a further Act 'for the encouraging the consumption of malted corn and for the better preventing the running [smuggling] of French and foreign Brandy' reinforced the first one. Queen Anne also cancelled the Distillers' Royal Charter. The most unscrupulous trader could sell whatever noxious spirit he cared to.

The English had become fairly familiar with gin, for long often called Hollands. Whether the coincidence that William III came from the Netherlands, birthplace of gin, played any part in the matter, or whether it was simply that English distillers knew little about making any other flavoured spirit, is conjectural. The facts are not. Consumption of gin was around 500,000 gallons in 1690. By 1727 it had risen to nearly 5,000,000 gallons. Some of this spirit may not truly have been gin, but that was the name attached to it. By 1733 London was producing 11,000,000 gallons, legally, and none knows how much illicitly. And gin was distilled in some other cities as well. Gin was the patriot's spirit; though 'Hollands' by type, the English metropolitan masses had adopted it wholeheartedly. Patriotism and inebriation went happily hand in hand.

The subject of this book being an aspect of social drinking, and since gin is crucial to the Dry Martini, I make no excuses for dilating on the social history of this particular spirit. I find it a fascinating rags-to-riches story. Who could have foreseen that this opiate of the toilers would end up as the cherished solace of the world's most civilized drinkers? For initially, only those who were – not without reason – called the Lower Orders, drank gin. It was despised by the upper classes, including those who mightily benefited by increased grain sales.

In due course, the nation's rulers awoke to the obvious: that the city workers were largely in a state of semi-permanent intoxication. This might affect their efficiency. That gin was a means of obtaining temporary relief from their almost intolerable living conditions was little considered, nor that they were ruining their health. Intemperance was endemic at all levels of society: people took as little notice of a reeling labourer as of a peer sitting blind drunk in Parliament. 'Magistrates often appeared on the bench heated with wine', records Sir George Trevelyan in his *English Social History*. But the proletariat must be prevented from excesses calculated to impair their labours and which possibly might lead to civic disorder.

To this end, in 1736 came the first of the Gin Acts, which aimed at removing gin from the orbit of the majority of the population, whilst raising some useful revenue. This Act was singularly ineffective, led to riots and to the production of a large quantity of inferior spirit which, not being technically gin, escaped the regulations. It was christened Parliamentary Brandy. The law was virtually unenforceable; juries were reluctant to convict, informers risked murder, fines went unpaid. Prohibition, by price or proscription, never works. The 1736 Act was repealed in 1743. In that year something like 20,000,000 gallons of gin were being produced in London, and most of it drunk there. The country's population was six and a half million, that of the capital around 500,000. Gin was essentially a metropolitan – mainly London – problem: the statistics show what a problem.

Bereft of the more impractical elements of the first Gin Act, one in 1751 placed a reasonable tax on gin and this measure did abate the worst of what serious historians call the Gin Era. Sensible regulations encouraged responsible distillers to produce sound gin and have pride in their wares: the only London distillers in business in 1751 that are still operating are Booth's, founded around 1740.

Not that gin was yet respectable; far from it. Though a former and much quoted sign on a Southwark grog-shop 'Drunk for one penny, dead drunk for tuppence, clean straw for nothing' had lost some validity, Hogarth's oft-reproduced, cautionary 'Gin Lane' struck a topical enough note. No longer did an estimated one in five houses in the Cities of London and Westminster purvey gin, nor could it legally be sold in any shop or hawked from door to door, yet consumption was enormous. However, the worst was over. Women of some gentility, who had in any event never copied their menfolk's insobriety, had discovered the merits of good gin: the first inklings of acceptability showed. Not yet in the drawing-room, somewhat surreptitiously gin entered the boudoir.

Countrymen had demonstrated no interest in spirits. They reaped the grain for Gin distilling: they drank grain when it was made into ale and, later, into beer. This was to change with the burgeoning of the Industrial Revolution. Increasingly, the farmworker left his leaky cottage in its bucolic setting in an unspoiled landscape, which was only idyllic for a few months a year, and set off for the smokey cities, where he could earn what at first seemed to him big money. In due course he moved into one of the 'new model dwellings' rising in serried rows in the shadow of the gaunt factories. No more the rural excitements of poaching rabbits, no more vegetable garden plot with perhaps a pig fattening for Christmas, no more convivial gatherings in the village ale-house. Toil even more arduous, infinitely more hazardous: amusements nil.

So, as the populations of the cities grew, it became worthwhile to cater for them by provision of places of public resort. These were the neighbourhood public houses, usually located at strategic crossroads. They came to be known as Gin Palaces, and of earlier examples the young Charles Dickens was scathing. They were to improve immensely, and despite their pejorative soubriquet they did not deserve the opprobrium they were to receive at the hands of those who took their liquor at home, club or residual coaching inn. The Gin Palace, achieving its apotheosis in the second half of the nineteenth century, filled an important social vacuum. To it, from his rather sordid family dwelling, or, in the instance of migrant single worker, from his abysmal lodging-house, could come the tired factory worker. In the Gin Palace were brightness, light, company – and booze, of course. But instead of sending out one of the children to get a gallon of beer or a pint of gin, the whole household could all go along to that haven of neighbourly felicity on the corner. The ruling class did not like Gin Palaces: mindless of history, they saw the workers enjoying themselves, squandering their hard-earned money which they should have been saving so as the parish should not be required to support more indigent old, and wasting time that might have been employed on self-education and the perusal of improving literature. A small but vociferous temperance movement abetted these critics. Gin was their particular enemy. Dickens's celebrated illustrator, the vitriolically talented George Cruickshank – one of the most ardent and intolerant of abolitionists, a reformed dipsomaniac – published extremely lurid anti-gin cartoons.

Yet, by mid-Victorian times, it was by no means unusual to have gin in the house, as is witnessed by elegant 'Hollands' decanters. In wealthier circles, gin was still essentially a woman's drink: Byron, always the iconoclast, is almost alone amongst prominent nineteenth-century men – possibly the only peer – to have sung its praises: 'gin and water is the source of all my inspiration'. Yet so great was the prejudice against gin that in some homes, after, say, a sewing session with friends, the lady of the house would resort to some such euphemism as 'Shall we now have a little white wine?' – which did not mean 'Let's drink a glass of Hock' but 'What about a slug of gin before we disperse.' The equivalent of today's, 'I'm dying for a Dry Martini; what about you?' Genteelness in this direc-

Modern communications come to a gem of a London Victorian 'gin palace'. In the Red Lion, Duke of York Street, St James's, John Doxat (right) is interviewed on the history of gin by Derek Cooper for a BBC-2 TV series on sundry British tastes which had their beginnings in other countries. The Red Lion has very fine engraved mirrors, typical of the best of those 'gin palaces' which helped gin towards general social approval. It is quite small for such an establishment and is much worth a visit by connoisseurs of pubs: but it gets very busy at the principal hours of refreshment.
(Photo courtesy of Allied Breweries)

tion reached its epitome with decanter labels inscribed 'Nig', so that even the word gin should not contaminate the home. That must have been done by the same people who decked piano legs in frilly pantaloons, nether extremities to them being as taboo as gin.

Gladstone, whose liberalism was sometimes more apparent than real, hated Gin Palaces. In 1871 he sought to halve their number in England and Wales. To the credit of the Church 'as by law established', in the House of Lords – which then considered itself the protector of the man in the street against the vagaries of the lower house – a bishop in opposing this Bill observed tartly that it was an intolerable infringement of the rights of the populace and that he would 'better see England free than England sober'. Outcry from an only partly enfranchised public, and possibly this episcopal criticism, caused Gladstone to withdraw the objectionable proposal. That did not prevent him from losing power at the next election. Part of his lengthy explanation for this defeat was that he had 'been borne down in a torrent of Gin'.

In gin's history, there now began to take place a change wholly significant to my main subject and without which there would never have been a Dry Martini cocktail. Towards the end of the century, leading distillers in London started to make a new style of gin, unsweetened. Hitherto, English gin – if we except the unflavoured coarse spirit put out to evade Gin Acts – had been of a pungent Geneva type, cordial gins of various sorts, and the sweet Old Tom Gin which lingered into our own times but which is now almost defunct. The divorce of Holland and London was about to be finalized. From Unsweetened, the name changed to Dry, and then to London Dry.

Not only was this new gin infinitely more delicate than earlier distillations, but it easily lent itself to mixing with other flavours. This made gin acceptable to cultivated palates. Other factors were at work. Wardrooms in Royal Navy ships had taken to drinking gin with medicinal bitters (Angostura), which was to be refined into 'pink gin'. Gin had been exported from London early in the nineteenth century. In many parts of the Empire it had been discovered as going admirably with quinine-water, a specific against malaria: this became the gin-and-tonic. High imperial officials, returning to honoured retirement

Part of the still-room in the modern gin distillery of London's oldest-established distillers. There are in all seven stills, and the flavouring still second from right was first installed in Booth's old Red Lion Distillery in 1828, over eighty years after the family entered the gin business. The old distillery was badly damaged in the 1940 Blitz and the present one was opened in 1959. On the right are the condensers. In the immediate foreground the head distiller takes a sample from a 'spirit safe', the first of many exercises in quality control.

in Cheltenham, Bath or Tunbridge Wells, brought back with them their gin-drinking habits, giving unwonted respectability to the spirit. Juniper's therapeutic value had never been forgotten: gin was a pleasing way to absorb this salubrious essence. Growing feminine emancipation spurred gin's universal acceptance. With the coming of luxurious transatlantic liners, rich Americans poured into Europe, bringing with them new notions of drinking: the smarter ones imbibed gin cocktails. An amused Old World emulated this strange custom. By 1900, gin had completed its arduous progress, emerging gloriously as London Dry Gin.

Gin was now about to achieve another triumph, destined to sweep the world of fashion: the Dry Martini.

Production note

As I have previously indicated, gin is a universal product; some 'gins' (and the quotation marks are often well-earned) are of distinctly dubious provenance. Avoid them. Amongst top brands there is considerable variation in techniques; there are subtle differences in formulae. To synthetize distillation of the highest quality London Dry Gin – whether a product of London or of London controlled production elsewhere – I have taken a description written by a leading expert, from Booth's Distilleries. Though priding myself as a ginocologist, I could not hope to better it:

London Dry Gin is the product of the re-distillation of specially rectified spirit with natural flavourings known as botanicals.
There are three basic essentials which contribute to the character of a London Dry Gin. The rectified spirit which must be free from impurities, the distiller's choice and variety of botanicals and the design and control of the pot still used by the gin distiller.
Rectified spirit, as the name implies, is the product of a multi-column still. This eliminates, by distillation, those congenerics which give a product like whisky its character and flavour, but which needs maturing time in cask before it can be marketed. The character and flavour of gin is produced by re-distilling specially rectified spirit with botanicals and can be marketed immediately after manufacture. The essential botanical of gin is the Juniper

Berry. Amongst other botanicals used by gin distillers are Coriander seed, Angelica Root, Calamus Root, Cassia Bark, Cinnamon Bark, Lemon Peel, Liquorice, Orange Peel.
The variety and proportions of botanicals used are the closely guarded secret of each gin distiller. These, together with the design of his still and the control of his distillation process gives his product its distinctive characteristics.
Gin distillation is a batch process carried out in copper pot stills. After the required quantities of rectified spirit and botanicals have been placed in the still it is heated, usually by steam coils, to bring the contents to the boil. As the contents vaporize they are flavoured by the botanicals and in passing through a condenser change back to a liquid and become a gin distillate.
The art of a gin distiller rests in controlling the rate of flow of the still and in determining which part of the distillate is suitable for the gin he is producing. In the initial stages of distillation the output of the still is discarded.

Violgincello

This part of the still run is termed 'heads' and is collected in a feints receiver. When the distillate has the flavour required by the distiller's formula the output is run into a gin reciver. Control over the quality of the distillate is maintained by constant nosing and regular sampling for alcoholic strength. As the distillation proceeds the nose and the alcoholic strength change. From these changes the gin distiller can determine the point at which the distillate is no longer suitable for his gin. The final part of the still run is termed 'tails' and this is diverted into the feints receiver along with the 'heads'.

The contents of the gin receiver are thoroughly mixed by rousing with compressed air and a further sample for both quality and strength is then taken to ensure that the batch of gin is up to standard. It is then pumped to the bottling vat where its strength is reduced to the market requirement. This is done with demineralized water which, whilst reducing the alcoholic strength, does not alter the flavour of the gin which the art of the distiller has created.

7. Italy's Gift to the World's Dry Martinians - Vermouth

Signor Alessio was despondent. He had brought the secret of beneficient *vermutwein* from Bavaria, and it had found sufficient favour at the French royal court to have its name gallicized to vermout. This maceration of wormwood flowers in wine was certainly an improvement on previous draughts of this established herbal vermifuge, combining medication with a degree of social drinking. But high society of the early seventeenth century was fickle: Paris had not widely taken to Alessio's vermout and the fortune he envisaged attaining remained nebulous. He packed his bags and returned to his native Piedmont. Did France thus lose the chance of becoming the original home of vermouth?

I suggest it would be correct to date the true establishment of the vermouth industry – modern vermouth as we understand it – from a much later period, 1840, when was enforced the first rigorous control of its production in the world's vermouth capital, Turin. Seeking to ensure that no Italian vermouths unjustifiably carried indication of Piedmontese origin, and to guarantee quality, King Carlo Alberto issued licences requiring those who wished to sell *Torino* vermouth to prove their rights to that esteemed designation. The first such licence was granted to the company now celebrated as Martini & Rossi.

It is frequently stated – with more romanticism than fact – that vermouth stems from the legendary potion

invented, *c.* 500 BC, by Hippocrates. In his memoirs, which he penned before lapsing into obscurity, Alessio followed this tradition by calling his discovery *vinum Hippocraticum* – as did the ancient Romans. The virtues of essence of wormwood were known to medieval primitive medical science: the dietary habits of our ancestors ensured that intestinal parasites were an endemic complaint and search for specifics against their debilitating ravages was constant. *Vermutwein* evidently was a rediscovery, and refinement, of a very old drink.

As I have said, we do not know if it was due to Alessio – I would like to think so and thus gain him belated fame – that vermouth came to Piedmont, but it was sufficiently known by 1678 for Leonardo Fiorvanti to write: 'Vermouth is an aid to the digestion; it purifies the blood, induces sound slumber, and rejoices the heart.' (I use the later international spelling of vermouth, to which the English contributed the superfluous terminal aspirate.) This and other references indicate that vermouth was leaving the doctor's dispensary for broader fields.

It was not only on the Continent that a type of 'vermouth' was drunk long before its commercial introduction in Italy. That man of electic curiosity, Samuel Pepys, wrote in his diary of 26 January 1663: 'Up and by water with Sir W. Batten to White Hall, drinking a glass of wormwood wine . . .' On 26 February two years later, he recorded 'drinking a draft of wormwood wine' in the same company.

Commenting on this in *Drinking With Pepys* (Macmillan, 1963), Oscar A. Mendelsohn, Australian author of several drink books – including (in my opinion) the most valuable concise dictionary in its field – comments that Pepys and his Admiralty colleague were almost certainly drinking medicinally. But, equally obviously, the beverage was not displeasing or the diarist would surely have added critical comment. The wine was probably sweetened with honey and flavoured with herbs, a common practice with wines, particularly if as was often the case – they had started to oxydize and become vinegary. The addition of bitter wormwood would have produced a not unpalatable prototype vermouth, its dryness depending on how much was employed.

Vermouthorgan

The oldest-established vermouth house dates from 1757, but it is generally conceded that the earliest 'brand' of vermouth came out in 1786. Until then Italian drinkers called for their own 'prescription' – so much *vermout* concentrate to a glass of wine: much as we might specify so much vermouth in proportion to gin in our Dry Martinis. If the current recipe for the original branded vermouth, Carpano's *Punt e Mes*, is similar to the original, late eighteenth-century taste was for a bitter-sweet vermouth. From this developed the somewhat sweeter, less bitter *rosso* vermouth which popularized vermouth in Italy, France, Britain, and eventually universally.

Piedmont was particularly well-endowed for the making of vermouth. The white wines of the region provided a perfect base and its hillsides were rich in herbs. As formulae for brands of vermouth became more elaborate and standardized, the Turin area was strategically placed to obtain imported ingredients through the great commercial port of Genoa or via Venice, famed for its trade in exotic botanicals from the orient. Recipes from the past, listing as many as two hundred ingredients, are on record at the Martini & Rossi museum. Today, the number is more likely to be around a quarter of that.

As a robust, fortified wine, vermouth comfortably maintained its original character when exported and, once established commercially, its popularity soon spread round the world. In more modern times it has been produced – at its best under Italian auspices – in many countries.

Historically, vermouth was the traditional *rosso* (red) variety – subtly sweet with a mildly sharp after-taste. But around 1800, in the Marseilles region of France, a new style of vermouth made its appearance. This was a dry vermouth, virtually without sugar, based on the thin, somewhat tart, wines of the Midi. Its principal use was in the Vermouth-Cassis (Vermouth and sweet alcoholic blackcurrant cordial) which became a favourite aperitif drink throughout France. Because of its origin, dry

The finest panoramic views of central London can be seen by those fortunate enough to be invited to the fabulous Martini Terrace, one of several such centres run by Martini & Rossi in great cities. Either the lady in our picture is enjoying a real man-sized Dry Martini, or – as I suspect – she's having an iced Martini Extra Dry, and her lucky companion is having the cocktail with gin.

vermouth came to be called 'French' to differentiate it from the original 'Italian' type. A mixture of the two also found considerable favour. It was the English who started drinking vermouth with gin; firstly with 'Italian' (Gin-and-It) and then, with 'French' (in more sophisticated circles). Gin-and-mixed (with equal proportions of the two Vermouths) was popular when I was an adolescent.

However, the division of vermouths by nationalities no longer makes sense. Large quantities of *rosso* vermouth are produced in France; a great deal of dry vermouth is made in Italy: the most important extra dry vermouth bears a world-famous Italian name. (The issue is somewhat confused by a modern vogue for *bianco*, the blonde extra-sweet Italian vermouth. That really has no bearing on this book, and neither do the various Chambéry vermouths from French Savoy – excellent on their own as aperitifs – yet one can hardly ignore their existence when speaking of vermouth.) Elsewhere in this book I shall employ only the terms dry vermouth and, occasionally, red vermouth.

It is, of course, dry vermouth that is essential to our subject. It has a respectable history, and is a direct linear descendant of the *vermout* of that little-sung Piedmontese adventurer, Alessio. He would but faintly recognize his vinous progeny – but let us drink a Dry Martini cocktail to his memory.

Production note

Needless to say, there are widespread divergencies in the making of vermouth, but these are the general principles in the land which gave birth to it. Infusions of the sundry herbal ingredients, according to the brand's formula, are prepared. The essential merits of some herbs are best extracted by mixing with water, others with alcohol. Simple maceration may be used, steeping the ingredients in appropriate liquid for a considerable period; by rotating them in drums to speed flavour extraction, and, in some

A small section of the plant where many herbal ingredients are compounded for the delicate flavouring of vermouth in the great Martini & Rossi installation near Turin, focal point of the company's world-wide production facilities.

cases, by distillation. The resultant concentrated flavours will be drawn from the remaining solids and stored. Piedmont no longer produces anything like enough wine to support the Italian industry and huge quantities come from the south which produces just the right sort of white wine. It is an illusion to believe that any wine will do: quality matured wine is used. The wine is very thoroughly filtered and then the blended flavourings are introduced, together with grape spirit. (Sugar and colouring are added for red and bianco vermouths.) When wine and flavourings are thoroughly 'married', the vermouth is subjected to refrigeration, about minus 10°C, which causes any deposits to precipitate to the base of the vats. Pasteurization and further filtering take place prior to bottling. Vermouth can stand remarkable temperature changes and retains its flavour perfectly for a considerable time after opening: but I do recommend that, when a bottle of extra dry has been half-used, the remainder be transferred to a smaller vessel.

8. Interlude

A Literary Curiosity

I have been criticized by some who have read parts of this book prior to publication for being too prosaic about the invention of the Dry Martini. Where's the *mystique*? they have demanded. The Dry Martini is a drink but, they say, it is also a living legend, redolent of runes and incantations. In delving for truth, have I lost the romance?

Well, I cannot alter the facts, yet I have been persuaded to break pace at this juncture with a digression from the serious tone which, I trust, informs most of this work.

In this endeavour I have been singularly fortunate – indeed the co-incidence might defy credence by a sceptic – in fortuitously coming across a rare literary curiosity with a direct bearing on our subject. It casts entirely new light – historical and whimsical – on the derivation of the Dry Martini. I feel it deserves place alongside my more mundane observations.

It may be that readers themselves have come across other unpublished material. In that event, I would be glad to receive copies (not originals) with a view to possible publication – subject to the owner's approval – in future editions.

BOSWELL ON BOOZE

From *The Life of Samuel Johnson, LLD*, by James Boswell – the world's most celebrated biography:

BOSWELL: 'You know, sir, drinking drives away care and makes us forget whatever is disagreeable. Would you not allow a man to drink for that reason?'
JOHNSON: 'Yes, sir, if he sat next to you.'*

The great Dr Johnson constantly referred to drinking matters, both favourably and censoriously. In modern times a considerable quantity of Boswell's papers, hitherto thought lost, have come to light. Mostly they have concerned his personal life, but evidently the following dialogue was intended for inclusion in the 'Life' but was mislaid. It was written on two and a half sheets of paper and was lately discovered in the pages of a very boring old volume on philately picked up from a second-hand barrow in London by my friend Harry Kovaire. This is possibly a valuable discovery, but Mr Kovaire – known in his small circle as the world's least-published author – refuses to part with it. For some reason which, typically, he refuses to divulge, even money cannot tempt him. He has kindly given me the opportunity to copy the document, and I take his word for its authenticity.

Where the manuscript starts, Boswell is enthusiastically dilating on the attractions of a new type of Italian wine he has tasted.

JOHNSON: 'Pray, sir, if this wine be flavoured with wormwood, a prime specific, is it not rather a nostrum than a wine?'
BOSWELL: 'Since it is pleasing to the palate, sir, how may it be a medicinal? Effective palliatives must be vile of odour and taste, for such is a law of the physicians.'
JOHNSON: 'Sir, I enunciate the witticisms in this company. To continue, if your wine be not evil in flavour, it must by its nature be bitter.'
BOSWELL: 'In some taverns, I have heard it called Dry.'

*Boswell originally attributed this question to 'a gentleman'. Authorities later established that it was he himself who posed it. Obviously, Boswell, who was rather vain, made the attribution anonymous because of Johnson's rude riposte.

JOHNSON: 'Sir, to talk of a dry liquid is as logical as to speak of a flat globe.'
BOSWELL: 'It is a new mode of description, sir.'

Dr. Johnson bade me obtain some of this wine, which I purchased from a Piedmontese merchant named Martini. I could scarcely credit it when the man informed me that some London bucks are mixing this wine with the juniper flavoured Hollands that is commonly, under the vernacular title Gin, the favoured tipple of the rougher people. To this concoction the popinjays of St. James's and its environs add the essence from the skin of lemons. They say it has stimulating and appetising virtues.
I took the wine to Dr. Johnson's house. He sniffed it, yet, this being one of his periods of temperance, would not drink it despite my protestations of its excellence. I told him what signor Martini had said of the strange manner in which some gay blades were employing this beverage.

JOHNSON: 'Sir, to add ardent spirits to wine smacks of alcoholic hyperbole. It would be a veritable cocktail of a drink.'
BOSWELL: 'A cocktail, sir? Pray, what is that?'
JOHNSON: 'In parts of the country, sir, it is a bucolic custom to dock the tails of certain horses of merit, yet which are not of entirely pure stock. Such animals of mixed provenance are then known as Cocktails.'
BOSWELL: 'It requires a distinguished lexicographer to uncover such a word.'

Dr. Johnson did not acknowledge my compliment, but I think he was pleased, for he continued in the same vein.

JOHNSON: 'Now, sir, since we have aptly applied an item of esoteric equine nomenclature to this peculiar mixture, may we not further designate it amongst potables, along with the worthy Negus and Shrub? You applied to the wine the anhydrous adjective Dry, which is a contradiction in terms and thus may properly be applied to this Cocktail that defies normality and which I deem no honest English potman would willingly serve, devoted as he and his ilk may be to the gin which is one of its constituents. You say that the purveyor whence you obtained the unusual product of

the grape is named Martini. Thus shall we, sir, call this presumptuous vinous conceit the Dry Martini, a ridiculous name for an absurd commixture which will certainly prove but an ephemeral fashion with idle fops, and which, I trust, sir, you will henceforward ignore as too frivolous for a man of parts.'

BOSWELL: 'Yet, sir, you have devoted some time to discussing it.'

JOHNSON: 'When a man awaits his dinner, sir, it is soothing to contemplate trivia.'

We then went to table, yet I was determined, despite the good doctor's directive, to test this enticing. . . .

Unfortunately, the manuscript finished here, so we shall never know how Boswell fared – unless the missing pages turn up.

9. In search of an Ideal - Martini Fact and Folklore

Mr Alec Waugh, in writing about the merits of the Martinis he used to drink in Tangier, says that while Scottish guests of his were drinking one of these admirable cocktails, the wife said to her husband, 'I wonder if they put into this the two drops of rose-water you recommend?' That was manifestly this man's notion of an ideal Dry Martini. Or should I have reserved this strange addition for my chapter on Mutations? For every Dry Martinian has his own idea of the ideal, be it but in some small addendum or a tiny detail in the preparation. When I was helping to entertain Japanese Bartenders in London, we invited some of them to mix Dry Martinis, and I particularly remember one man who put a drop of Angostura bitters at the top of the mixing spoon and let it dribble down into the ice as he stirred. I wouldn't put Angostura into a Dry Martini: yet it would be sheer pedantry to condemn the practice, if that's the way it's liked in Tokyo or Yokohama. Fashion, local or international, must affect minutiae of Dry Martini lore: to have unchangeable *law* would be to consign the Martini to the fate of the dinosaur. It is a living cocktail.

Mr B. C. Carlton-Jones, wine merchant of London, reminds me that when Beatrice Lillie, appearing on stage as 'Aunt Mame', showed her nephew how to make a Martini, she poured an entire bottle of dry vermouth into a jug and emptied it out of a window into the garden, refilling the jug with gin. Since I am about to risk giving my *own* ideal Dry Martini, I quote this happy conceit since I partially endorse its extravagance. Into a mixing glass – see Tools Of The Craft – half-filled with large ice cubes, I pour 4 ounces of Martini Extra Dry vermouth. When it has reached the base of the glass, I strain this off and discard it. Immediately, I pour in, per serving, at least 2 ounces of Booth's High & Dry gin. I stir very briskly for approximately thirty seconds and strain into pre-chilled stemmed goblets. Over the top of each glass I press fairly large slivers of lemon rind, cut from a fresh (washed) lemon, which must be a soft, supple one not an old hard number. I do not immerse the peel, nor do I use olives – but we'll come to that later. Speed is the essence of the contract, and everything must be to hand.

You may say that this is an ultra-dry Martini, in the 25:1 range. It is not: a quite surprising amount of vermouth clings to the ice. I like the subtle hint of the vermouth. To paraphrase the old Martini joke: 'If I want an iced gin, I'll ask for one.' This must necessarily be an opinionated chapter, and I'll go on record as saying that Martinis are, in many quarters, becoming too dry. By using minute quantities – or no – vermouth some people are missing something, without realizing it. I do feel it is time, in the progressing Martini story, that we ceased to shun that dry vermouth which made the Dry Martini in the first place; that we abandon this super-dry syndrome, and return closer to the 7:1 Booth's Martini which was listed as *Ideal* by no less an authority than David Embury.

You notice I am against immersion of the lemon peel. Visually, some people like this because it gives colour to the mix – after going as far as possible to make it a-chromatic (even, in extreme instances, to the use of totally colourless vermouth – though this was a, mainly dis-continued, practice allowing some bartenders to cut back on the gin). My objection to total immersion – which I consider a religious, not a bar, ritual – stems from the imparting of too citrus a flavour.

The addition of a green olive is purely optional, and a tradition which is on its way out in my observation. I don't see it adds anything, and only reminds me of the story of the chap in a New York bar – or it may have been Los Angeles – who sat drinking Martinis, and each time he had one he put the olive aside on a plate, which he guarded carefully. After this had gone on for some time, and the chap was distinctly the better for wear, another customer asked the bartender what was going on. 'I don't know,' was the answer, 'all he's told me is that his wife sent him out to buy a bottle of olives.'

My 'ideal' Martini will not be received with enthusiasm by several of my bartender friends – at least, not by those who remain traditionalists. They say a dash of orange bitters is essential to the classic Dry Martini. I find professional opinion (I write from Britain) about evenly divided on this issue. I opine that bitters were once an obligatory part of the mix, but that their use is archaic. A majority of modern, not older, cocktail books are on my side. Frankly, unless you overdo them, I don't think bitters make much difference – but my friend Gerry Kelly, of the snug little Vine Bar in Piccadilly Place, London, will be rude to me after he reads this!

When we come to preparation, there's considerable diversity of opinion. Kingsley Amis, who is all for the convenience of the host, thinks that it's more important for a Dry Martini to be very cold than very strong. He stirs vigorously 'for about a minute' (see his *On Drink*) and leaves the mix to stand for two or three minutes whilst he gets out his refrigerated glasses, into which he drops a piece of lemon rind: he admits that he hasn't mastered the knack (?) of squeezing this to release the magical, almost invisible, oil. He then stirs again, and pours. If you have any left, he says, providing you remove the ice, you can put this into the refrigerator against the next round. (David Embury is dead set against this advice: he says you can no more refrigerate a Martini than you can a kiss.) Quite rightly, in a contribution to *Penthouse*, Kingsley states that a 'diluted Martini is better than a tepid Martini' – but I think his dilution is excessive. In

A TINY SQUEEZE OF LEMON RIND
FREEZE THE SHAKER
JUST A 'BREATH' OF VERMOUTH!
STIRRED NOT SHAKEN
A SPATTER OF PERNOD, OLD BOY
A DASH OF ORANGE BITTERS
DON'T BRUISE THE GIN!
WITH A TEENY WEENY OLIVE
LOTS OF ICE
MAKE IT TWO
A SLIVER OF LEMON
TAKE OUT THE ICE
NO VERMOUTH
JUST GIN AND VERMOUTH
AND A MORSEL OF CHEESE
CAN I HAVE A CORGITAIL?

Martyranny

the same feature, Kingsley said he prefers Martini Extra Dry for vermouth and Booth's Gin, the company's traditional and unique style, much relished in the U.K. by gin connoisseurs. Remember, this gin was also given by Mr Embury as his own favourite. In fact, Mr Embury called a Martini made with this gin a Golden Martini, anattractive description. To reiterate my personal preference – the old ego will break out – I opt for the clear, *very* delicate High & Dry for Martinis, reserving Booth's Finest Dry for drinking straight with a little chilled water: it does wonders in keeping my gout at bay!

The demand by that very popular bounder, James Bond, for a Martini 'shaken not stirred' sent a quaver through Dry Martinian circles. It had long been a part of the faithful's credo that to shake a Martini was a form of alcoholic blasphemy, a desecration of bibulous piety, which – in a once popular phrase – 'bruises the gin' or 'bruises the vermouth' – both of which robust products can take a good deal of punishment. There is no practical reason why a Martini should not be shaken: in fact, it will speed both dilution and refrigeration. But it is, for most people, aesthetically displeasing and it offends the rule that only cocktails containing fruit juices and cordials need shaking in order properly to marry them with the spirits. Nor, to Dry Martinian ears, can the rattle of cubes in metal match the delicious music of ice tinkling in a well-handled mixing glass. Not that a shaken Martini was any new thing when Ian Fleming's egregious hero committed his alleged gaffe. Mr Embury refers to a shaken Martini as a Bradford. He doesn't say whence comes the peculiar name, certainly not from the famous Yorkshire city which, for all its virtues, has never been noted for its contributions to mixology. Evidence of the longevity of Dry Martini shaking as opposed to stirring may be found in the first edition of the famous *Savoy Cocktail Book*, with recipes codified by the great Harry Craddock. (In 1965 this was revised to accord with modern practice and re-issued: it is still in print – and has

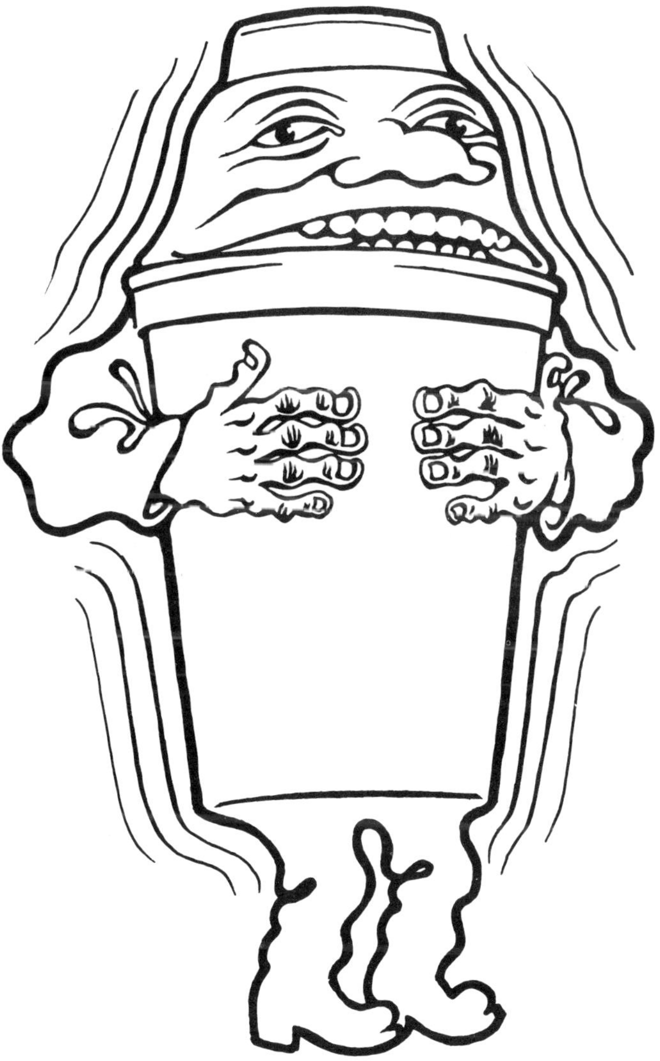

been translated into Japanese!) Harry was brought over from the U.S.A. as Prohibition hit that country and when the Savoy opened a cocktail bar which, of course, survives as one of the capital's smartest places. Harry's original sole recipe for a Dry Martini called for half-and-half French vermouth and gin with a dash of orange bitters: 'Shake well and strain into cocktail glass.' No mention of lemon rind or olive.

On the rocks

In fact, for a Martini-on-the-rocks, shaking is not a bad method. The contents of the shaker can be poured entire into the awaiting glass. Sometimes this, now entirely legitimate, style of Dry Martini is made with cubes, sometimes with crushed ice. The latter is not easy to drink in comfort – one can hardly drink a Dry Martini through a straw! An advantage of the on-the-rocks procedure, against the trad 'straight up', is quick dilution – and thus postponement of intoxication – and, for those who wish it, more intense coldness.

The search for frigidity reaches absurdity when people put a dash of vermouth in a bottle of gin and place it in a deep freeze for a time: the result is only technically a Dry Martini, and is ridiculously strong. The same occurs, though refrigeration is less formidable, by the use of water-filled globes which are frozen and dropped into the mixing glass: no dilution at all. Subtle breaking down of the gin with ice is generally held crucial to a good Dry Martini, let alone an ideal one. This was not a view shared by Mr Epps, formerly omnipotent butler at the London residence of the American ambassador, according to a correspondent of mine, Mr Cecil W. F. de Brandt, export consultant to the wine trade. Epps's idea of a Dry Martini was to put a bit of lemon peel in a bottle of export strength gin and store it in a refrigerator. Ambassadorial Dry Martinis were made by putting a few drops of dry vermouth in a glass, tossing them out – rather as one would with bitters in making a pink gin – and topping the glass up with the ice-cold spirit. Writing to Ambassador Douglas, prior to one of his trips to London, then Secretary of State, the late Dean Acheson, remembering prior occasions, requested that at any event he might be attending a more conservative recipe be employed.

In connection with various matters of detail, it is relevant to quote from a remarkable spoof document, of which a copy was sent me by Mr John Stace, of The Distillers Company Limited, London. It was published under the sponsorship of the 'Water Conservation League' and bears the imprint – 'Approved August 31, 1966, by American Standards Association. (This is the last American Standard.)' Its full title is *American Standard Safety Code and Requirements for Dry Martinis.* A lot of thought went into this work – of which the humour is as dry as the subject – together with a profound knowledge of, and love for, the cocktail. Surprisingly, it condemns the use of lemon peel under a series of definitions, viz. 'Lemonade: a term applied to drinks which have been subjected to the peel of a lemon. There is no place for the rind of any citrus fruit, or its oils, in an American Standard dry martini.'

An olive is considered optional: 'The absence of an olive is not critical provided there is no diminution of the total volume of the drink.' Since 1966, there has been a considerable growth in the Dry Martini-on-the-rocks habit. It is condemned outright: 'Rocks. The solid state of H2O, on which an American Standard Dry Martini is never served.' Vodka, too, gets the bullet: 'It is never employed in a dry martini.' The document obtains my approval when laying down sizes: 'The American Standard Dry Martini shall come in the following three sizes: (1) Regular – not less than 3½ ounces. (2) Large – not less than 5 ounces. (3) Double – not less than 7 ounces.'

To recapitulate, the ideal Dry Martini will contain the best of gin and vermouth. In regard to the latter, there will be no nonsense with atomizers or any form of spray or aerosol. Refrigeration will be sensibly applied by direct contact with ice. The drink will be mixed expertly; no gimmickry. The whole subject will be approached without reverence, or chi-chi, but with dignity: we are in the presence of the noblest concoction devised by man to illuminate the social scene.

10. The Mutations: the Sound and the Outlandish

When Marilyn Monroe was once asked what she wore in bed, she replied that her sole slumber accessory was Chanel No. 5. It may have been this much-publicized statement which impelled those in search of exotic Dry Martiniana to use this celebrated perfume in place of vermouth – or this abberation may have occurred at an earlier date. I don't know: I only quote the anecdote to indicate the absurdities which will radiate from any rite, be it a religious or bibulous one.

Though I have seen such ridiculous recipes listed as one for a Bronx made with whiskey, the fact is that, alone of famous cocktails, the Dry Martini, in its long success story, has spawned a number of excellent mutations, without the main stream becoming unduly polluted. Purists may argue that I should ignore these, but I am convinced they have their place here: a few deserve recognition in their own right and none need deflect a Dry Martinian from the true faith. To maintain that the classic Dry Martini itself is immutable is to defy the lessons of history.

By far the most popular mutation is the Dry Martini in which Vodka is substituted for Gin – the Vodkatini – an acceptable heresy which has indeed in some areas gained ascendency. So much so that I could be accused of failure in omitting vodka from my list of 'Essentials': I did so in the cause of orthodoxy; I am, by nature, one of the orthodoxats!

By all means let us explain vodka. The word itself is a version of the Russian equivalent of *eau-de-vie*, i.e. distilled spirit. It was invented, medicinally of course, some eight hundred years ago in Russia or Poland (according to which book you consult) and it has long been produced in those countries, in all Slav territory, in much of Scandinavia, in the Balkans and as far east as Persia. In its native habitat vodka is a generic term for spirits. I have seen a report on the Leningrad vodka factory which gave thirty-two types of vodka as being made there. The flavour range was from red pepper to chocolate: different vodkas for varying purposes and to suit regional tastes.

No purely geographical meaning attaches to vodka; unlike Scotch whisky, the word itself carries no precise connotation of origin. So far as the western world is concerned, vodka began its meteoric career in California in the late 1940s – strangely enough at a period when the Cold War between the U.S.A. and the U.S.S.R. was at its most frigid. Contrary to all expert prognostications, vodka quickly swept across the land, and then jumped to Britain, to Europe and to many countries hitherto totally unfamiliar with it.

When referring to vodka, it is essential to appreciate that there are decided differences, in flavour and production methods, between the spirits produced in countries where vodka is the traditional drink of ancient lineage and the modern vodka which I dub as the Anglo-American style. Traditional vodka I designate for descriptive convenience as the Slav type. The lighter ones that are exported are meritorious spirits deserving attention: the best way to drink them is neat, very cold, accompanied by (someone else's) caviar or smoked salmon, or, in my estimation best of all, by smoked salmon rolls stuffed with caviar. Russian and Polish flavoured vodkas are rarely used for Dry Martinis. As a mutation, a Moscowtini does not rate high with me: too much, and wrong, taste in the spirit. As Kingsley Amis says – keep your Russian or Polish vodka for other purposes.

By contrast, the distillers of Anglo-American vodkas aim to put out a spirit of great purity without any flavour at all other than that inherent in the alcohol. This renders them a dull drink to take in the traditional Russian way – but makes them a splendid base for many mixed drinks. In passing I should say that I know of a rather attractive lemon-flavoured vodka (Old Bailey) sold in the United States – though produced in London – which will make what I feel I must call a Citrontini: don't add any lemon rind.

From now on, when I refer to vodka I mean unflavoured vodka.

To return to the Vodkatini. Customarily, this is mixed exactly as one would make a traditional Dry Martini, merely substituting vodka for gin. Personally, I find this lacks something: I miss the delicate aroma of the gin, which does not dominate the mix but adds an essential essence. So my advice to those who are dedicated to vodka is that for Vodkatinis they increase the proportion of vermouth. I go as far as using one-quarter vermouth to three-quarters vodka. No insipidness there. Some American authorities support me: for a Vodka Gibson, the *Esquire Drink Book* gives two jiggers vodka to a half-jigger of vermouth: I return to the Gibson anon.

I will be immodest enough to believe I have made a worthwhile contribution to Dry Martini mutations. This is the Cossacktini, consisting of 3 ounces Cossack vodka, 1 ounce Martini Extra Dry vermouth, prepared in a mixing glass in the usual way – very well iced – and strained into a substantial stemmed glass. Then squeeze over the top a fairly large slice of grapefruit (not lemon) rind: don't immerse it.

Kingsley Amis, whom I have occasion to quote many times – *not* because he contributed an Aperitif but because he talks good sense on spirits and their uses and is opinionated without pedantry – in his fine little book *On Drink* published an interesting Vodkatini, called Lucky Jim after his famous novel. It is made with '12 or 15 parts Vodka, 1 part dry vermouth, 2 parts cucumber juice, cucumber slices'. He says you can easily produce cucumber juice by using a fruit-squeezer. The mixing is as for a Dry Martini, and I reckon this is an instance where shaking might be better than mixing. The cucumber slices floating on top of the drink are unpeeled. 'It looks unusual, rather mysterious in fact: faintly coloured and faintly cloudy, the green wine of the Chinese emperors come to vigorous life,' wrote its inventor.

Mutations of the Dry Martini have been produced using all sorts of spirits – aquavit, white rum, arrack, tequila. The last-named was inevitable, as the pungent Mexican spirit made its surprising gains in the U.S.A. I can take them hardly more seriously than such subversions as Martinis made with sherry in place of vermouth or sundry other substitutes including pastis. It is difficult to draw the line where a variation ends and a quite different drink begins: obviously a 'Whiskey Martini' would be half-way to a Manhattan. I must try to deal with mutations without getting excessively involved in permutations.

Perhaps not a mutation at all but a return to the past is the Martinez cocktail listed by Trader Vic in *Bartender's Guide*, an up-dating of the Jerry Thomas recipe that caused so much subsequent confusion. It is 3–4 ounces gin, 3–4 ounces dry vermouth, ½ teaspoon each orange bitters and curaçao. An interesting compromise between Jerry's sweet mix and today's Dry Martini.

Earlier I made brief reference to the Gibson. It is arguable if this is a mutation at all; just a minor alteration to the classic form. But there is a subtle modulation of flavour. I need hardly say that a Gibson is a Martini plus a pearl onion in place of the optional olive; the twist of lemon should not be dropped in – excessive garbage.

I had been under the impression that this version of Dry Martini came into being in the following circumstances. During Prohibition, which coincided with the burgeoning of the Cocktail Age, an American ambassador was at pains to follow his country's laws whilst abroad but did not feel he should deprive of alcoholic sustenance the guests he entertained in the country to which he was accredited. In order to set them at ease as he circulated at diplomatic cocktail receptions, an intelligent aide suggest-

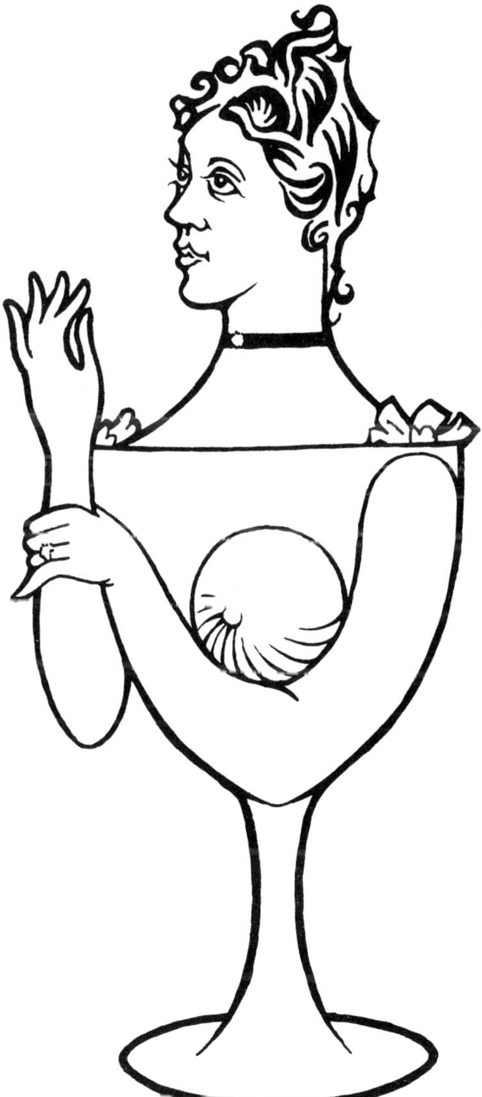

ed that the envoy carry a small glass of iced water, given the semblance of a cocktail by embellishment with an onion on a stick. Asked what their host was drinking, this aide replied that it was a Gibson, named after the ambassador, and was a Dry Martini with this special addition. Any new form of cocktail, or change to an established one, was at that period much sought after: so the ambassadorial custom was adopted and spread outward to a wider social circle. Legend probably, but an attractive one. It has been effectively destroyed for me by Mr John McCarthy, of Rye, New York – appropriately named home-town for one well-versed in potables. His tale is a much more likely one. During Prohibition, Charles Dana Gibson, the celebrated American artist who created the Gibson Girl, dropped into his New York City club, The Players, and asked Charley Connolly, the bartender, to mix him 'a better Martini'. The Connolly answer was to mix one with a little onion substituted for the usual olive. Gibson enthused over the mix – and the Gibson was born.

You may ask how this happened during Prohibition? The Players club was, and is, a resort of persons of talent in the arts who, when it was founded by the famous actor Edwin Booth – whose father emigrated from England – were for various reasons not acceptable, nor wholly at ease, in some circles. Edwin's brother it was who had assassinated Lincoln and it was then normal socially to visit a man's sins on his family. (Incidentally, he was not remotely related to the famous Booth family in London, England's oldest-established gin distillers.) Members of The Players were scarcely people to allow governmental insanity to deprive them of alcohol. So, during the dry years, they gave over the bar to Connolly to run privately as an exclusive speakeasy. Charley became wealthy, yet when Prohibition ended he returned to his legal position as steward: he only recently retired and shortly afterwards died. John McCarthy tells me a good Gibson tale. A few years ago, he had the well-known Irish actor, Cyril Cusack, as his guest at The Players, and Charley Connolly made him a superb Gibson. Cyril Cusack took the recipe to

Dublin and asked the owner of Murphy's Bar, a favourite resort of his, to repeat it. Murphy made up a mix of mostly gin, a touch of vermouth and a radish instead of an onion. 'That's a Murphy, not a Gibson!' said the actor. And 'tis said that the 'Murphy' is still drunk in Murphy's – but I haven't been to check.

Opponents of the Gibson have been known to refer to it as A.O.S. (Alcoholic Onion Soup) – an amusing libel.

It is doubtful if a Sweet Martini (made with gin and red vermouth) has any right in this book, but a Medium Martini which, for reasons I cannot explain, some authorities list as the Perfect Martini may be acceptable to those for whom the Dry Martini is too dry. It is made in the same way, but the vermouth is half sweet and half dry. David Embury, that foremost of cocktail-men, gives a dash of both orange and Angostura bitters as part of the recipe. Commenting on the use of the word 'perfect' in this connection, he says that whoever first applied this name was a poor judge of mixed drinks, just as 'whoever named near-beer was a bad judge of distance'.

Mr Embury lists a Martini de Luxe made with 1 part Lillet to 7 parts gin. I hate to fault him, but he calls Lillet a vermouth: it is not; it's a distinctive aperitif wine, and this mix is as great a distortion as the use of sherry. If rare nomenclature excites you, Mr Embury has these names for Dry Martinis with certain additions: with a few dashes of curaçao, a Flying Dutchman Martini; ditto of Chartreuse, a Nome Martini; with pastis, an International Martini, which may alternatively have a few dashes of crème de cassis or Benedictine. A medium Martini with a couple of dashes of absinthe (not widely obtainable) is a Bald Head Martini; with two dashes of kümmel, an Allies Martini; with a dash of anisette a Deep Sea Martini and with two dashes of both absinthe and grenadine, a Gloom Chaser Martini. . . . For what is certainly the most comprehensive list of mutations, I think I should refer you to Mr Embury's *The Fine Art of Mixing Drinks* – which no enthusiast should be without – for definitions of these Martinis: Parisian, Hong Kong, Yale Fence (with applejack); Cooperstown; Boomerang; Lamb's Club; and numerous others. The mind boggles at Mr Embury's erudition and imagination.

The Naked Martini, under that name, was first brought to my attention as being served in a Florida bar: It was Booth's (House of Lords) gin, iced as for a Dry Martini proper but without any vermouth. Effectively, this is simply straight gin (though rather special gin), whether or not it has a twist of lemon or an olive. I like neat gin very much, but I am wary of including it even in this annexe to the Martini pantheon. It's popular, but *is* it a Martini? Reluctantly, I give it the benefit of the doubt – an extreme mutation. Tony Rocque tells me that before he retired from Quaglino's, London, he had an American in the bar who was concerned that his Martini should be really dry. 'Don't worry, sir,' said Tony, 'I'll make you a Streaker.'

'What the hell's a *Streaker*?'

'A naked Martini, sir, no vermouth.'

I have some marvellous glasses which were specially introduced in the U.S.A. to bring the merits of imported Booth's gin to a wider audience: rather like large brandy balloons, they are great for a gin on the rocks, for which they were designed. They, and the drink, are called Snifterinis. For a mammoth Dry Martini they are sensational – if you want a quarter-pint Martini. Now there's a man's drink for you! I've managed one – once.

That drinks which are only faintly reminiscent of the real thing should bear the title 'Martini' is a great compliment to the Dry Martini. I suppose that every day, somewhere, someone is coming up with a new deviation from the mainline Dry Martini. None can be more extraordinary than the Martinicicle, said to have been obtainable in New York City, which is a Dry Martini under such intense refrigeration that it comes out in the form of a lollipop on a stick. To lick it would be to leave half your tongue behind. Yet I've had that sensation in some ordinary bars!

'St Genevieve with a touch of St Martina, lots of St Frigidian, stirred with an apostle spoon'.

Stirred – Not Shaken

A Dry Martini – London dry gin, Turin Vermouth, Israeli lemon and frozen Pellegrino ice in a Swedish glass stirred with a Welsh gold spoon – no Spanish olive

11. International Scene

Within the following pages will be found a selection of bars in various countries – some widely famous, others of more localized renown. I have in certain instances added comment about the establishment and its bartender, and other fairly pertinent information. In no way is this section intended to be a survey of the world's leading cocktail bars – it aspires to do no more than to illustrate the universality of the Dry Martini; though all the places are worthy ones, inclusion is not meant to confer a special accolade any more than, of necessity, many notable omissions imply disrespect.

AUSTRALIA

Austrian-born Heinz Gross, head barman of the San Francisco Grill Bar, Sydney, claims that martinis are one of the most popular drinks in his bar. And the way Heinz makes a martini, that's not surprising.

Always stirred (*not* shaken) and presented in individual glass pitchers encased in an ice-filled bowl, Heinz's martinis are based on a very generous quantity of gin with a dash of extra dry vermouth. Heinz recalls his best martini effort being on a private yacht anchored in Montego Bay, Jamaica. A group of international jet setters had been invited on board, and Heinz was asked to prepare a pre-dinner drink for the guests.

He placed a crystal jug in a large silver bowl filled with crushed ice. Into a second jug went five large pieces of ice, three good dashes of vermouth and a large bottle of gin. Heinz gently stirred his super-martini, and strained it into the prepared jug. Olives in chilled silver bowls were scattered around the room.

MARTINI
HIGH & DRY
BOOTH'S
DRY GIN
750 ml

AUSTRALIA

It may surprise some visitors to find a Pakistani serving Dry Martinis in a smart bar in Brisbane. However, the credentials of Akhtar Sethi, bartender of the Crest International, are impeccable. He first trained and worked in the Dorchester, London, before transferring to the Curzon Club. After thirteen years' London experience he moved to Australia.

Akhtar gained fame in mixing circles during a visit to the city by Gina Lollabrigida, the much-photographed beauty who has turned out to be a beautiful photographer. A competition was organized between twenty-two bartenders to find a cocktail most to Gina's taste: Akhtar won.

When it comes to Dry Martinis, Akhtar favours the technique of pouring off any residual vermouth before adding the gin to the ice in the mixing glass.

IGH & DRY
BOOTH
DRY GIN
M·R

AUSTRALIA

Full marks to the Hilton Hotel, Melbourne, for employing a woman as head bartender – Miss Sharyn Hayes. She was also the first overseas lady member of the United Kingdom Bartenders' Guild, an admirable organization in many ways, but, until the British Sex Discrimination Act loomed, a bastion of unwarranted male chauvinism. Sharyn only started her brilliant mixing career in 1971, in Lennons Hotel, Brisbane, later helping to open their Lennons Plaza. She then went to Sydney, running the Crest's bar; then the new Terrace Bar at the Sheraton. Going on to Melbourne, she first worked for the Southern Cross and joined the Hilton in 1974.

Sharyn has developed strong views on Dry Martinis. Unless specifically requested otherwise – and she stresses that any customer's preference is of paramount importance – she sprinkles vermouth in the mixing glass and discards any surplus, before adding ice and the gin. When a twist of lemon is called for, she believes in igniting the oil before dropping the twist into the drink. She claims this emphasizes the flavour. Well, that must make a good discussion point with some ardently opinionated Dry Martinians.

MR
MARTINI & ROSSI
HIGH & DRY
BOOTH'S
EXTRA DRY
VERMOUTH
MARTINI ROSSI

AUSTRIA

Kurt Pinter, of the Intermezzo Bar at the Vienna Intercontinental, makes many traditional Dry Martinis. But he had at least one customer, an important businessman, who would ask for a Tutti Frutti – a very dry Martini embellished with olive, pearl onion and lemon rind.

BELGIUM

There are peculiarities of Belgian licensing laws which it is not my function – nor do I have the space – to explain. This complicates the situation vis-à-vis cocktail bars. For example, on Brussels' famed Grand'Place, in the Maison du Cygne, the Bar de l'Ommegang officially is part of a select private club, where Albert Lahaye presides as head bartender. Albert, a virtuoso mixer, has won several international prizes.

BELGIUM

'Le Cerf' is a very old private house – a status it preserves technically today – and was probably built in 1710. It was one of the few patrician residences on the Grand'Place, Brussels, at a time when nearly all houses were owned by trade guilds. It is remarkably well preserved, full of period furnishings. Jean-Marie Bertrand is seen in Martini-action in the fashionable cocktail bar. The list of fine liquor it stocks is formidable, and I can only fault it on the omission of Hine from the cognac list.

BRAZIL

On the Martini Terrace in São Paulo, Armando Skarlovaj, the well-known bartender who comes from Trieste: winner of the 1975 Paissa Prize for the best cocktail.

The 'Piero Paissa' prize was established by Martini & Rossi, in memory of one of their executives who died prematurely and who was specially interested in training young Italian bartenders. It was later extended worldwide under the auspices of the Martini International Club.

BRAZIL

Brazil possesses many smart cocktail bars and Brazilians seem fond of Dry Martini anecdotes. McCann-Erickson, on behalf of their client, Martini & Rossi, have sent me several: I append two.

Two slightly inebriated customers are chatting vociferously at Michel's in Rio de Janeiro.

'Waiter, a Dry Martini!'
'And so, you too have lived in São Paulo. What a coincidence! In what district?'
'Higienopolis.'
'You're kidding! I also lived in Higienopolis. Waiter, another Dry Martini . . . On what street did you live?'
'Sabara.'
'Impossible! The same street. When did you live there?'
'A very long time ago – 1960.'
'Incredible! We must celebrate that. Waiter, another Dry Martini. And now we must check the street number.'
'Of course. I lived at 342.'
'No, it's not possible!'
By this time, the whole restaurant are listening attentively. One bald gentleman asks the waiter who those two peculiar men are.
'Oh, it's nothing. Something like that always happens when this man and his son get together for a few Martinis.'

Wearing dark glasses and a wide-brimmed hat pulled over his forehead, the mysterious gentleman enters the Green Room of the São Paulo Hilton. He chooses the least visible table, and as the waiter approaches, he whispers:

'Waiter, bring me a Dry Martini. But be as discreet as possible, because I must *remain incognito.'*
Calmly and quietly, the waiter serves one, two, three Dry Martinis. The gentleman then writes a cheque and quickly leaves.
A few seconds later, the waiter catches up with him:
'I am very sorry, sir, but it seems you've forgotten to sign this cheque.'
The man turns angrily to the waiter. He looks nervously around, then whispers:
'I thought I told you, I must remain incognito.'

Miss Universe savours a Dry Martini on the São Paulo Martini Terrace.

CANADA

Canada is, like the U.S.A. able to employ for Dry Martinis gin distilled in the country by British companies which has all the qualities associated with London Dry gin produced in the English capital itself. Thus it is at the S.R.O. Room of the Hyatt Regency Hotel, Toronto, where Roy Whitson is the senior bartender.

DENMARK

Jens Thornbaek, in the bar of the Kong Frederik, Copenhagen

EAST AFRICA

The world-famous Tree Tops hotel in Kenya is a sophisticated 'water hole' whence, uniquely, you can watch elephants – and other wild-life – enjoying themselves at a genuine African water hole whilst you drink a Dry Martini. No wonder head bartender Wilson Mutoku calls his Martinis 'Jumbotinis'.

EAST AFRICA

A Dry Martini being a fine 'sun-downer', in Nairobi residents and tourists alike flock to the Safari Bar in the New Stanley Hotel, where Mohamed, the head bartender, an adroit mixer, is a well-known local character.

FRANCE

I have not meant to be impolite to the celebrated Harry's New York Bar, one of the bibulous delights of Paris, when I suggested that its peculiar and delightful ambience was not, to *my* mind, quite right for ingestation of Dry Martinis but rather for serious drinking of the straight hard stuff. In fact, it is noted for its Dry Martinis, and opposite we see Bob preparing a good and strong one. Harry's Bar is the only place where I have seen Frenchmen imbibing Dry Martinis in large quantities – though when I first frequented the establishment in the thirties it was quite rare to find any Parisians there.

Harry's is probably the first true American-style cocktail bar to be opened in Europe which is still flourishing. Established in 1911, it soon achieved fame, with expatriate Americans (and tourists) in particular, as 'sank roo doe noo', the phonetic spelling of its address in adequate – for taxi-drivers – if imperfect French. It added to the world's repertoire two classic and enduring cocktails, the White Lady and the Sidecar. In 1924, height of the Cocktail Age, the International Bar Flies club was founded in Harry's. No drinker, visiting Paris, should fail to visit Harry's: the Martinis are as American as New York.

FRANCE (overleaf)

Ultra-modern, ultra-chic is the Concorde Lafayette, in the bar of which Michel is seen in action.

FRANCE (page 109)

The Georges V was the first luxury hotel to be built in Paris after World War I, on the avenue of the same name – which had formerly been the Avenue de L'Allemagne. It had one of the earliest of Parisian hotel cocktail bars and from its opening it was a resort of the rich and famous cosmopolitan set. Ninno now presides over the bar.

Stirred – Not Shaken

BOOTH
MARTINI

GREAT BRITAIN

In the delightful Pine Bar of the Britannia Hotel in London's Grosvenor Square, the author discusses the merits of a High & Dry Martini with head bartender Peter Burbidge.
Note: *I should not be holding the glass by the bowl but by the stem. However, it wasn't given time to get warm! J.D.*

BRITISH AIRWAYS

In the first-class lounges of British Airways' 747s, Dry Martinis are easily the favourite mixed drink, according to Flight Purser Ron (Snowy) Philpott. First-class passengers get them free – and decidedly large. An ex-chairman of the Guild of Sommeliers, 'Snowy' is also from time to time a senior instructor for British Airways cabin staff trainees. As this book goes to press he will probably be looking after people hurtling between Washington and London in Concorde.

Stirred – Not Shaken

Dry Martini around the world

BOOTHS
FINEST
GIN
BOTHA

GREAT BRITAIN

In my personal introduction to this book I have mentioned the Dorchester, London, in an hotel context. In the frivolous thirties, with my late rich friend, Perico Claude, I often watched the cabaret acts in the Dorchester restaurant. Yet, strangely, though I drank a lake of Dry Martinis with Perico, I do not recall the Dorchester's bar in those days. In modern times I have certainly repaired any omission, as can be vouched for by Roy Adcock, pictured opposite in action – and if the photo does not do him credit you can blame me: I took it.

Roy joined the staff of the Dorchester as a pageboy when it opened in 1931 as the last word in luxury hotels, a status it has maintained by constant renovation – without affecting the special Dorchester ambience. This was summed up for me by a charming American couple who, after a world tour – during which they stayed in the greatest hotels of many countries – gave their preference as the Dorchester: Service was why they awarded it top rating. The Dorchester is a totally independent hotel, and its independence is reflected in its style. And this style is epitomized in the bar. Here Roy has worked since 1935, becoming head bartender in 1952. Recently redecorated for the fifth time, the bar is a haven of good taste, with its own entrance from Park Lane, and – very importantly for serious vertical drinkers – has a long bar counter on which one can lean whilst enjoying one of Roy's fine Dry Martinis. He reckons that 80 per cent of all cocktails ordered at the Dorchester are Dry Martinis – a higher proportion than in any bar I know personally. Of these, more are asked for on-the-rocks than straight-up – the Dorchester is much frequented by discerning Americans; the British prefer the latter variety. At least one-third of Roy's Dry Martinis are made with vodka – again an indication of American influence. I don't think Roy – as big in heart as he is small in inches – will mind me saying that the splendid Dorchester Grill is the one restaurant in London where I would confidently order a Dry Martini at table; head sommelier Luigi Averono is an adept mixer. But I admit to preferring a bar situation for my Martini-izing.

HIGH DRY
LONDON DRY GIN
MART

GREAT BRITAIN

Asked to name England's premier seaside hotel, a very high proportion of knowledgeable persons would certainly say the Imperial, Torquay. In 1976, this enduring and renowned establishment celebrated its 110th anniversary. Napoleon III stayed there with his son, the Prince Imperial and expressed delight in the cuisine. No surprise there, for the chef had previously worked in the Emperor's kitchens in Paris. As Prince of Wales, *bon vivant* Edward VII paid several visits from his yacht, and the steps leading to the hotel from the landing-stage bear his name.

The Imperial's gastronomic reputation has survived, and is epitomized in the Gastronomic Weekends, held regularly, which attract gourmets from near and far away. Certainly, many of these cognoscenti of good living repair to the cocktail bar for a Dry Martini or two before a lucullan repast, sharing with me a belief that the Martini is the finest of appetizers. In the bar, with luck, they will find Dennis Eldergill presiding: he is pictured opposite.

Dennis has been well over thirty years at the Imperial, for almost the past twenty of them as head bartender. Serving as he does an élite clientele, he goes for ultra-dry Martinis – about 99 per cent gin or vodka – but even then he can't satisfy everyone. Knowing one woman to like her mix as dry as possible, he decided to serve it without any vermouth at all – what is known as a Naked Martini. Perhaps predictably, back came the complaint, 'not dry enough'.

'One must remember odd personal quirks,' says Dennis. 'In the old days, for Eugene Higgins, the American millionaire, I had to add a dash of Angostura, Prince Bertil of Sweden liked a dash of Pernod in his Martinis.'

Dennis is seemingly ambidextrous: his right hand mixes the Martini, while simultaneously his left hand rotates ice in the glasses to chill them.

HIGH & DRY

GREAT BRITAIN

The Leofric, Coventry, which some claim to be the top modern metropolitan hotel of Britain's industrial Midlands, has only had one head bartender since it opened in 1955. He is my friend Ray Rastall, and it was not long before the hotel's owners named the principal cocktail bar Ray's Bar – and rightly. Displayed are the numerous trophies that Ray – pictured in action opposite – has won in major cocktail competitions, and he has been highly placed in many more. Unusually – at least for a British bar – there's a fine oil painting of him, which Ray thinks gives the bar special personality. I agree. Ray ascribes his widespread reputation in his craft to 'dedication. Whilst you must always retain the old standards of service, you must look to the future for mixing cocktails to interest the younger generation.' But, of course, the Dry Martini will always be there.

The Leofric was the first major hotel to be built in Britain, outside London, after World War II, and set a style which no later ones have exceeded in my much-travelled estimation. It stands in the centre of the city, close to the proud ruins of the ancient cathedral and the controversial new one, and the hotel epitomizes Coventry – so war-ravaged – which combines imaginative (and, for a change, successful) town planning with surviving antiquities. Personally, I can't understand why the hotel was not named the Hotel Godiva – the famous Lady's statue stands just outside it – rather than after her lesser-known tyrannical husband: it would have given Ray the opportunity to specialize in 'Naked Martinis'.

Like all good bartenders, Ray believes a Martini should be made the way the customer prefers, and is never shocked. The nearest he came to being so was when he produced a perfect 'on the rocks' for a client who tasted, expressed appreciation, and then added soda-water to it.

U.K.B.G.
COCKTAIL
COMPETITION
NATIONAL FINALS
TORQUAY
MARTINI
MARTINI
MARTINI
Black & White
BEEFEATER
MARTINI

HOLLAND

Cees Iske at work in the Pulitzer Hotel, Amsterdam, restored from fifteen seventeenth-century buildings in the city's centre. Latterly, Mr Iske has been promoted from chief bartender to a managerial post.

HONG KONG

The Dragon Boat Bar, Hong Kong Hilton

INDIA

Presiding over the Lancer's Bar at the Oberoi Sheraton Hotel, Bombay, is Babbi Ahluwalia, a Sikh.

HIGH & DRY
BOOTH'S

IRELAND

The four bars of the Gresham Hotel, Dublin, come under the control of Jerry Fitzpatrick, seen opposite in the Aperitif Bar, the establishment's latest. He was a founder member of the Irish branch of the United Kingdom Bartenders' Guild and is now its president. With thirty years' experience in the hotel and bar trade, Jerry has seen Dry Martinis change. He finds his customers increasingly like around three ounces of gin on the rocks with a dash of dry vermouth, which he remembers making years ago, but then bitters were employed; not so today. He has been asked to add a teaspoon of brine from a jar of cocktail onions to a Dry Martini – and has complied, though I doubt if he much cared for doing so. Dry sherry has also replaced vermouth with some customers; I have myself found this done, but only during immediate postwar shortage of good vermouth. Jerry approves of lighting a twist of lemon peel about the drink and letting burnt oil drop on to it.

MARTINI
HIGH & DRY
MARTINI

ITALY

Oscar Rabitte, of the Ristorante Savini in Milan says that when he prepared a Dry Martini for James (shaken not stirred) Bond – Sean Connery – he always dropped a large olive into the glass. Mr Connery would always politely say, 'Please, Oscar, I want to drink, not eat.'

HIGH & DRY
BOOTH'S
LONDON DRY GIN
MARTINI
MARTINI
VERMOUTH
SECCO
V5

ITALY

Two particular customers are recalled with special affection by Mauro Lotti, of the Grand Hotel, Rome, illustrated opposite. For Tennessee Williams Mauro always prepared Dry Martinis with olives. These were not for the famous author but for his small dog, which was adept at jumping on to the bar stool and taking the cocktail stick delicately between its teeth, jumping to the floor and demolishing the olive. Mauro recalls the pet as a 'very pleasant animal, with green eyes' – presumably to match the olives.

In a previous position at the Beau Rivage, Lausanne, Mauro used to serve the late Somerset Maugham, a devotee of Dry Martinis, when he came there after his regular visits to Professor Niehans' clinic. 'He used to drink a Dry Martini as if it were a rite, and he tasted it in the same way he enjoyed his cigarettes, without filter, and smoked to the last bit held with fingers tired and yellowed, that looked almost golden.'

ITALY

Ulisse Troglia, of the Hotel Principe di Savoia, Milan.

NEW ZEALAND

Allegedly, Bob Clements of the Sporting Life Bar, Intercontinental Hotel, Auckland, makes his Dry Martinis by throwing some dry vermouth into the air and catching a few random drops in his mixing glass before adding the spirit!

NEW ZEALAND

The Marine Bar of the United Service Hotel, overlooking the main central square of Christchurch, is always used by the celebrated British Lions touring rugby team: but they probably drink more beer than Dry Martinis. However, bartender Chris Jenner is renowned for his – and if anyone dares say they aren't dry enough, he jokingly suggests they strain them through a towel!

MARTINI
BOOTH'S

QE2 CUNARD

Ronnie J. Stammers, *QE2* bartender – seen in action opposite – was born in Southampton in 1930. He began his career in 1947 aboard the *Aquitania*. Having worked in the *Caronia* for a short term, he moved to the *Mauritania* – the ship he was with for fifteen years. Before joining the *QE2* in May 1969, the preceding four years were spent with the *Queen Elizabeth*.

Basically, he mixes two Dry Martinis:

1. 8 parts gin; 1 part Martini Dry; twist of lemon or an olive. This is mainly for Americans.
2. ½ gin; ½ Martini – virtually Signor Martini's original, less the bitters he used.

Ronnie Stammers recalls that the late Mr Kruschev is said to have described the American Martini as the U.S.A.'s most lethal weapon.

CUNARD
HIGH & DRY
BOOTH'S

SOUTH AFRICA

South Africans in Natal prefer their Dry Martinis in the traditional 'straight-up' style – with a twist of lemon and a green olive – according to Gilbert (the name is pronounced *à la francaise*) of the Causerie Cocktail Bar in the smart The Edward Hotel, Durban. The hotel being situated opposite one of the city's main Indian Ocean beaches, patrons – dehydrated by the sub-tropical sunshine – haven't far to stroll for a cooling drink. But popular as it is as a holiday resort, Durban, the country's largest port, attracts many businessmen and it is probably for them that Gilbert, pictured in action opposite, makes the majority of his Dry Martinis.

South Africa is a major producer of fine spirits. The best gin, such as the High & Dry favoured by Gilbert, is distilled to the same formula and quality as that produced in London. In recent times there has been a considerable interest in vodka, though it is doubtful if the Vodkatini has caught on to the extent it has in some countries, and straight cane spirit is also very popular.

(Photograph by courtesy of the Southern Sun Hotel Group)

HIGH & DRY
BOOTH'S
London Dry Gin
MARTINI
VERMOUTH
SECCO
MARTINI ROSSI

SOUTH AFRICA

It seems that the hot, dry climate of sophisticated Johannesburg generates a demand for Dry Martinis on-the-rocks. That's the opinion of Christopher Noone (see opposite), bartender in Churchill's Bar of the Landdrost Hotel, flagship of South Africa's largest chain, the Southern Sun Group of Hotels. One need hardly explain the bar's title: obviously it commemorates Winston Churchill's exploits during the Anglo-Boer War when, as a war correspondent, he was captured and later escaped. Landdrost needs more explanation for the uninitiated: it is the old Dutch word for magistrate, a man much required to keep order in the 'good old days' of the original gold boom, an era reflected in the bar's furnishing.

This is a very popular watering place with businessmen of South Africa's commercial centre. Christopher favours a large green olive in the Dry Martinis he builds for them.

HIGH & DRY
BOOTH'S

SOUTH AFRICA

Martin, head bartender in Cape Town's Heerengracht Hotel, presides over the Van Donck Room. This bar, atop one of the city's tallest buildings, can claim as spectacular a view as is enjoyed by drinkers anywhere. The bar is named after the legendary sea captain who, according to a local myth, challenged Satan to a pipe-smoking contest, and whenever clouds mask Devil's Peak – which can be seen from the Van Donck Room – they say the two nicotian competitors are continuing their rivalry.

The hotel's title translates, from the old Dutch, as Gentleman's Walk, once the main street of the original settlement, and lies close to the spot where Jan Van Riebeeck landed in 1652 to establish the first permanent colony in South Africa: due to foreshore reclaiming, the site is now some way inland.

Martin likes to differentiate between the Dry Martinis he makes for customers of different nationalities, an admirably commonsense approach. For Americans it's a 10–1 gin/vermouth ratio; for local residents something nearer a more classical 2–1.

MARTINI
HIGH & DRY
BOOTH'S
London Dry Gin

SPAIN

José Farrerons of the Sandor Hotel, Barcelona speaks about 'The Martini Route' which consists of Dry Martinians moving from bar to bar to compare the subtle differences between his and other bartenders' mixing.

BOOTH'S
HIGH & DRY
EXTRA DRY GIN
MARTINI
VERMOUTH
MARTINI

SPAIN

A good (true, for a change) Dry Martini story is told by Enrique Bastante – of the Hotel Henry, Madrid. It is not easy to translate some anecdotes but I'll try:

Henry was serving a Martini to Ava Gardner, and as he poured her drink, a customer called his surname, 'Bastante!' to attract his attention. ('Bastante' is Spanish for 'enough'.) Quick as a flash, Ava, who speaks the language fluently, said, 'It may be enough for him – but I want more!'

MARTINI
VERMOUTH
SECCO
MARTINI & ROSSI
BOOTH'S
HIGH & DRY
EXTRA DRY GIN
BOOTH'S DISTILLERIES, LTD.

U.S.A.

Peter Carlson operating in New York's celebrated Laurent Restaurant. Peter must be one of very few bartenders to have attended the Mormon's Brigham Young University.

U.S.A.

Primo Carpana has run the bar of The Bistro, New York City, for over a quarter of a century, and before that he worked at the St Regis Hotel, so he's very much part of the city's cocktail circuit. He's a long-term devotee of what is sometimes called the High & Dry Martini. Frank first trained under Fernand Petiot who is said to have originated the Bloody Mary.

U.S.A.

Harry Max at work at the Clayton Inn Hotel, Clayton, Missouri.

U.S.A.

In St Louis, Missouri, when customers ask Clyde Lovelace for a Dry Martini at the Chase Park Plaza, they are getting one mixed by a man with around forty years' experience.

U.S.A.

In that most beguiling of American magazines for the bon vivant, Gourmet, *I have read mouth-watering descriptions of the fare at Chasen's, the establishment opened by the late comedian Dave Chasen with the help of the* New Yorker *magazine's founder, Harold Ross. It has achieved the very difficult feat of being both a mecca for celebrities and a temple of gastronomy, and if I ever find myself in Beverly Hills I shall certainly eat there (hopefully at my publisher's expense) – but not before I've had a couple of bumper Martinis made by Pepe Olivas.*

U.S.A.

The Carnelian Room, San Francisco, is located on the 52nd floor of the Bank of America building, and our picture gives just a notion of the spectacular views from it over city and bay. Locally it is widely rated the best restaurant in San Francisco, a place noted for the quality of its cosmopolitan cuisine, and it has been put to me it is the best in the whole U.S.A. – and those claims are made even though it is only open to the public in the evenings: during daytime it is reserved for members of the Bankers' Club of San Francisco.

It is not usual for an establishment which is part of a major group to enjoy such a high reputation, yet this restaurant is one of sixteen throughout the U.S.A. run by Davre's, of the ARA Food Service Corporation, one of the country's largest such organizations with over one billion dollars annual sales record.

To indicate the sensational situation of the bar, unusually, our photograph is taken from behind bartender Richard Williams as he prepares a Dry Martini directly on-the-rocks. In the background are Bob Simpson, restaurant and club bar manager; Miriam Moore (they didn't tell me who she is, but she must be important), Marvin Israel, general manager of the Carnelian Room, and his secretary, Marilyn Routh. Now guess who the Martini's for!

U.S.A.

*Jovanelo's is one of San Francisco's cosy, friendly 'in' places, owing its intimate atmosphere to the constant attention of the owner, Nello Piccinini, who is seen chatting to two customers, Vi Rodriguez (*left*) and Janine Loesch, while bartender Al Nannini appears to be topping up the boss's Dry Martini – not exactly orthodox practice, but Mr Piccinini does run a highly personalized establishment: he's named his special martini a 'Thigh Opener'.*

U.S.A.

*The Restaurant at the Merchandise Mart and Galleria Buildings, San Francisco, has a prime situation because through this complex pass thousands of trade show visitors in notoriously thirsty (and sometimes hungry) throngs. Owners of the restaurant, Mr and Mrs Henry Adams, are seen talking with Dan Ravetti (*left*), who runs the five bars in the Buildings and owns four of the city's largest licensed package stores.*

U.S.A.

I'd certainly like to have a Martini mixed by a restauranteur who looks as happy as René Martin, who with his wife Josie owns La Bastille. It would give one a glow before it had even been poured. La Bastille is a totally French outpost of gastronomy in an old house in north Chicago, but there's no nonsense about not starting a fine repast with a couple of Dry Martinis: Franco-American amity personified.

U.S.A.

If you can't get a splendid Dry Martini in a place named Martini's Restaurant, where the heck can you get one? Well you certainly can obtain one from Louis Giovanetti, partner with Albert Parenti in Martini's Restaurant, Grand Avenue, Chicago. They took over when Mr Martini, who opened the establishment shortly after repeal of Prohibition, retired. Chilling glasses with cracked ice is a very good method, Lou!

WEST GERMANY

Hamburg enjoys the reputation of a swinging city, and this is reflected in The Blue Satellite Bar on the twenty-fourth floor of the Hamburg Plaza, on Marseillerstrasse. As our picture shows, it is a far cry from the traditional German bar. When bartender Calvin Johnson was asked if he had any Dry Martini anecdotes, he couldn't recall one. My correspondents in the city say his only joke is unrepeatable! He's presided over this smart bar for sixteen years, and is a noted bartender, but his real love is Opera.

WEST GERMANY

Says Konstantin Stark, bartender at the King's Corner Bar at the Hotel Der Konigshof, Munich:

A barman who knows his job is a man who knows his world. Unfortunately, the majority of us do not work in our own places and the bars are designed according to the ideas of hotel or bar managers without asking the bartender. These people may have good reasons to act the way they do but chances are that the result does not conform to the bartender's personality. Look here, I like the warm and cosy type of bar; but this one is all plastic from top to toe. My place behind the bar is two steps lower than the floor before the bar. The chap who worked here before me was rather small. He could hardly reach up the glasses to where his customers were, to say nothing about the fact that a conversation is almost impossible unless two people are looking at each other at the same level!

Nevertheless I love my job. We, here in Munich, have a lot to do with films, fashions and literature. These people meet at regular intervals and they have a lot to discuss, but they always find the time to say some nice words to me. They call me by my first name and I am proud of it. Then, of course, beside those regulars, there are also numerous casuals. I don't like them particularly. They call me 'keeper' or even 'waiter' – in these cases I just don't listen; but if they call me 'garçon' I answer: 'This must be the man who worked here before me. My *name is Conny!'*

You ask me if I know a nice story about bar life: wait a minute! No I am afraid I don't. You know, I have been told lots of stories, and I nod or say 'yes' or 'no' or any colloquial sentence. The stories I don't really recall. The same with the many jokes I have heard.

There is just one gag I do remember – of the customer on whose lap the barman poured a good glass full of Dry Martini. The customer 'Look what you've done! I'm all wet now!' – the bartender: 'But that's impossible, sir. The Martini was absolutely dry!'

By the way; talking about Dry Martini; I think all that about the many official and 1001 secret recipes for a really good Dry Martini is nuts. Either you have the right proportions at your fingertips, or you have not. I flatter myself that I can produce a good Dry Martini, but I simply couldn't tell you how I do it. Many other bartenders know that too: nevertheless their Martinis taste different.

12. Thought for Food

Food snobs – whom no-one admits to being but quite a number of people are – and too many wine-lovers, tend to pontificate that the Dry Martini is not a suitable preprandial drink in the instance of any meal of merit. Such pedants, usually without much knowledge outside their own self-appointed expertise, pretend that so frigid and ardent an apertif concoction excoriates the taste buds, thus prejudicing appreciation of the rare viands in which (they imply) alone they find nourishment for their precious bodies. Further, they tend to opine that even the Dry Martini – quite apart from less distinguished cocktails – alarms the palate and renders it less susceptible than it might be to the charms of those exquisite vintages in which (it seems) they invariably drench their Lucullan repasts.

They are certainly entitled to their opinions, but let them not thrust them upon others. Persons of didactic nature in this matter, naturally have not for years – if ever – partaken of a Dry Martini, or have paid so little regard to its preparation that it has indeed ruined their evening. A little cool light sherry they allow themselves, a glass of chilled champagne or delicate dry white wine – but a cocktail; please don't be so vulgar!

I am not knocking wine: none enjoys it more than myself; though my gout is the better for gin. Indeed one great type of wine – fortified and aromatized – is crucial to my argument. I am attacking the anti-still clique, who seem to believe that no spirit exists outside a vintage cognac or long-aged Armagnac. If you like a Scotch-and-soda before a meal, or a gin-and-tonic – or a Dry Martini – insist on it and let not the viticultural babus dictate. It is akin to the notion so often promulgated by specialist gastronomic pundits that only such and such a style of wine may be drunk with certain dishes. There are no rules in eating and drinking but those of commonsense and individual preference.

Perhaps I've made my point. I'm not by any means saying that a Dry Martini is the *only* proper drink before a meal. I am not even saying you need a drink before a meal at all – though you will scarcely be reading this if you don't agree with me that it's a very pleasant habit. I am not saying that you will be better off for always having a Dry Martini before you eat. I *am* saying that if you're a Dry Martinian, habitually or occasionally, don't let anyone intimidate you from indulging your predelection.

At the risk of repeating myself, I will re-emphasize that the well-made Dry Martini is supreme amongst stimulant aperitifs in coaxing the gastric juices, in relaxing you for the pleasure of the table, in adding a cleansing and anticipatory relish to the comestible or vinous delights to come – or in providing armour against those culinary disappointments which are today all too frequently the fate of gourmet and gourmand alike.

Oscar Wilde said 'Enough is as good as a meal.' I have known more than enough Martinis turn an ordinary meal into a feast. Sufficient Martinis have preceded many of the most memorable repasts I have enjoyed. However, as I have elsewhere emphasized, discretion should be the soul of Martini-drinking. Know your capacity, and stick fairly closely by it. Again, Oscar said 'Nothing succeeds like excess.' Yet Martinian immoderation means social failure. So, should you be tempted by the peculiar savour of your own, or your host's, Martinis to exceed your normal limit, it is advisable to nibble at some dainty nourishment – such as is normally available at cocktail-time in either domiciliary or bar situations. You will do your ulcers a favour, giving the Martini something else to bite on. Nor will sensible ingestion of canapés impair appetite, for the cocktail will revive it. Should, in certain circumstances, the temptation to say 'Hit me again, Sam' become very strong, owing to Sam's singularly successful way with his mixing-glass, forego formal dinner (or lunch) but insist on substantial solids: I find smoked salmon sandwiches go extremely well with Martinis – brown bread, a touch of cayenne pepper, lemon juice at discretion. But if you are a Dry Martinian of any standing, you'll have your own ideas and need no advice from me.

13. Interlude - Alice at it again

Lewis Carroll made various amendments to his works. I am indebted to an acquaintance, Hugo Montmorency Jones, for the following extract from a little-known (pirated) edition – it bears no imprint – of the first 'Alice' book. He found this tome in the country mansion of a millionaire Socialist: knowing the library shelves to have been stocked by the yard with good bindings, regardless of contents, he felt no compunction in purloining it. Mr Jones, one of Britain's residual dilletantes, is an occasional contributor on recondite drink subjects to upper-class journals. For those concerned with genealogy, his name has a romantic origin. His father, Edmund Jones, owned a prosperous grocery business in Wales. Fairly early in life he suffered from the hallucination that he was a direct linear descendant of Henri, Duc de Montmorency, a leading character in turbulent mid-sixteenth-century France. No one could discover the origin of the mania – which got progressively worse – since Edmund Jones was not known to have read anything but the *News of the World*. He gave his son – his wife deserted him in the early stages of his dementia – what he considered a distinguished first name, which caused the boy, an only child, agonies at school. He willed Hugo a substantial fortune, and on his death-bed – in a moment of comparative lucidity as he expired from delirium tremens – exacted from his progeny a promise to preserve the 'family connection' by hereafter ever coupling the name Montmorency with that of Jones. Hugo made, and has kept, the promise in what he has described to me as 'a sentiment of filial gratitude not unmixed with social guilt'.

But we must return to Alice. The excerpt below is a complete incident which – unless it be an interpolation by a philistine hand – Charles Lutwidge Dodgson possibly considered too bibulous and thus erased from official copies.

Alice noticed a sort of bottle, with a label on it reading, 'Drink me.'

'Oh, not again!' she said aloud, for she was a trifle weary of random potions and their weird effects.

'Yes, again,' said the bottle.

'I was told never to drink from strange bottles,' said Alice, 'though I admit I have twice done so.'

'I am not a strange bottle,' said the odd glass object, 'I may be a peculiar bottle, but that is quite a different matter.'

'Yes,' said Alice, thoughtfully, 'in fact you don't really look like a bottle at all. More a sort of . . . I don't know.'

'Don't know! Of course you don't know,' retorted the sort of bottle. 'I haven't been invented yet.'

'Then may I ask what you are doing here?' asked Alice, haughtily.

'You may,' answered the s.o.b.

'What *are* you doing here?' persisted Alice.

'I thought you'd never ask,' said the s.o.b. 'I'm waiting for someone to drink me. Are you aged eighteen, or over?'

'Do I *look* eighteen?' demanded Alice, rather offended.

'Sometimes,' urbanely replied the s.o.b. 'On Sir John Tenniel's off-days. Or it may be his engraver's fault.'

'What has being eighteen got to do with anything?' asked Alice.

'Frankly, I'm not at all sure,' answered the s.o.b.

'Not having been invented is highly inconvenient. It's something to do with the law – but that hasn't been passed yet. And I'm getting warmer all the time,' it added, inconsequentially Alice thought.

'You're a bit of a mystery,' she said.

'I've been called that before – and since, I suppose,' said the s.o.b. a trifle sadly.

DRINK ME

Impetuously, Alice reached out and took the sort of bottle's sort of hand. It was decidedly frigid.

'You're positively icy!' she exclaimed.

'That's a highly personal remark,' said the s.o.b.

'I'm sorry,' apologised Alice, 'but it's true.'

'I only know I'm *supposed* to be cold – whatever I am going to be when I'm invented,' said the s.o.b. 'I withdraw my request about drinking me. We had better find someone older before I melt.'

Pulling on a mitten she conveniently found in her reticule, Alice took hold of the sort of bottle's sort of arm, and they started to walk through the wood. Quickly, they came upon a clearing.

'Oh, dear!' exclaimed Alice, 'that stupid tea party is still going on.'

'Perhaps we can jolly it up,' said the s.o.b. He half dragged Alice to the table.

'Ha!' shouted the Mad Hatter. 'I do believe we have here something more exciting than tea. Let's hold a cocktail party!'

'A *what*?' said Alice.

'That's me, that's me!' exclaimed the s.o.b. excitedly, as one recovering from amnesia. 'I'm no sort of bottle, I'm a cocktail mixer glass. Hurrah!'

'I think you're mad,' said Alice.

'No, I'm the mad one around here,' said the March Hare.

'No, *you're* not; I am,' said the Hatter.

The March Hare dipped his tea-cup into the Cocktail Mixer and poured the contents over the Dormouse. 'That'll wake you up, you sinister somnolent rodent,' he cried. He helped himself and served the Mad Hatter.

Alice watched in astonishment, and then in some alarm as the Dormouse started to execute a passable sword-dance on the table, using tea-spoons in place of the conventional weapons.

'You have just drunk the first Dry Martini,' announcd the Mad Hatter. 'My compliments to the Mixer.' He filled his hat from the obliging C.M. who was so happy at being invented and no longer being an s.o.b. that he did not care in the least that he was almost empty and quite warm.

'What on *earth* is a Dry Martini?' asked Alice.

'I haven't the foggiest idea,' replied the Mad Hatter.

'That's what's so marvellous about it.'

Alice glanced at the happy, glass-eyed C.M.

'But you said you haven't been invented,' she insisted, puzzled, but, as usual, appallingly logical.

'Of course, he hasn't been invented yet,' said the Mad Hatter, 'but there's no point in being in Wonderland if you can't anticipate things.'

They ignored Alice. As she walked on, rather thirsty as it happens, to another part of the wood, she distantly heard them singing, sadly out of tune,

'Twinkle, twinkle, little drink,
How you put me in the pink –
Cold and strong, and good and dry,
Nothing better 'neath the sky.'

14. Fantastical Martinis

These are not proper mutations, but rhyming names for the Dry Martini in particular or peculiar situations – actual, fictional or improbable: readers may care to add their own fancies to this initial list.

SPY MARTINI: the allegedly true instance of a Dry Martini with a 'bugged' olive, to pick up an espionage agent's conversation. But what happened if he ate it? The C.I.A. has declined to comment.

CRY MARTINI: The sixth or seventh successive double Dry Martini which sometimes induces sentimental or belligerent lachrymosity.

LIE MARTINI: The Dry Martini which a man tells his wife is his first that evening when in fact he's had two already.

NIGH MARTINI: Almost a cocktail – so weak, and insipid, as barely to qualify as a Dry Martini.

TRY MARTINI: If in quotation marks, this is advice to the love-lorn from a practical cynic. Otherwise it is the first, experimental Dry Martini in an unfamiliar bar.

FLY MARTINI: Exhortatory slogan composed, after lunch, by an advertising agency copy-writer who was having trouble with a new campaign for an airline.

THIGH MARTINI: The one that clumsy idiot on the bar stool next to yours knocks over so it soaks your trouser-leg.

FRY MARTINI: A tepid – or heated – Martini. Not recommended. Film star William Holden was reported as having managed to set fire to a Dry Martini: see *Fifty Years Decline and Fall of Hollywood* by Ezra Goodman. He dubbed it a Hot Martini – such a drink is calculated to hasten any decline.

MY MARTINI: As in, 'Just a moment, Buster, that's *my* Martini you're drinking!'

PIE MARTINI: The glass half-filled by vegetable matter – huge stuffed olive, outlandish onion, grotesque slice of lemon rind – leaving sparse space for liquor.

SLY MARTINI: Best example I saw of this was in the Hôtel Lotti, Paris. This American visitor, who evidently was no stranger to the bartender, came in and immediately a large Dry Martini and a glass of orange juice were put in front of him. He drank the Martini, glanced anxiously out into the foyer, then pointed at his glass. He received replenishment which he drank as one parched by the sands of Sahara. The bartender whipped away the empty glass. In about a minute a formidable matron arrived. 'Well, here you are. Are you ready?' she demanded loudly, casting a glance of disgust round the bar. 'Just let me finish my orange juice,' replied the hen-pecked but temporarily happy husband. I saw this repeated a couple of days later. Wonder what happened to the chap? Hope he took an axe to her and got away with justifiable homicide.

Speaking of orange juice – which I rarely do – reminds me of W. C. Fields and his flask of Dry Martini. He referred to this as his 'orange juice'. One day on the set some stage hands emptied the container and filled it with orange juice. Later came the stentorian Fields' trumpet: 'Who's been putting orange juice in my orange juice?'

PI MARTINI: Short for Pious Martini. Not correctly a Dry Martini cocktail at all, as it contains no gin: even worse than a Nigh Martini. But a perfectly acceptable drink if properly made and correctly named as a straight Extra Dry Vermouth, if chilled in a separate mixing glass, or as 'Martini Extra Dry on the rocks', which also indicates a preferred brand.

TIE MARTINI: A waste of money – you have spilled it on to your neckwear.

EYE MARTINI: A dangerous drink, signalized by failure to remove the stick of the olive which, should the glass be elevated hastily to the imbibing position may cause optical injury.

DRIVE MARTINI: The fourth or fifth double Dry Martini, after which one *must* NOT use one's car (except strictly as a passenger) for at least six hours – and then only after a substantial meal. If this advice is not heeded, the cocktail may become the terminal DIE MARTINI.

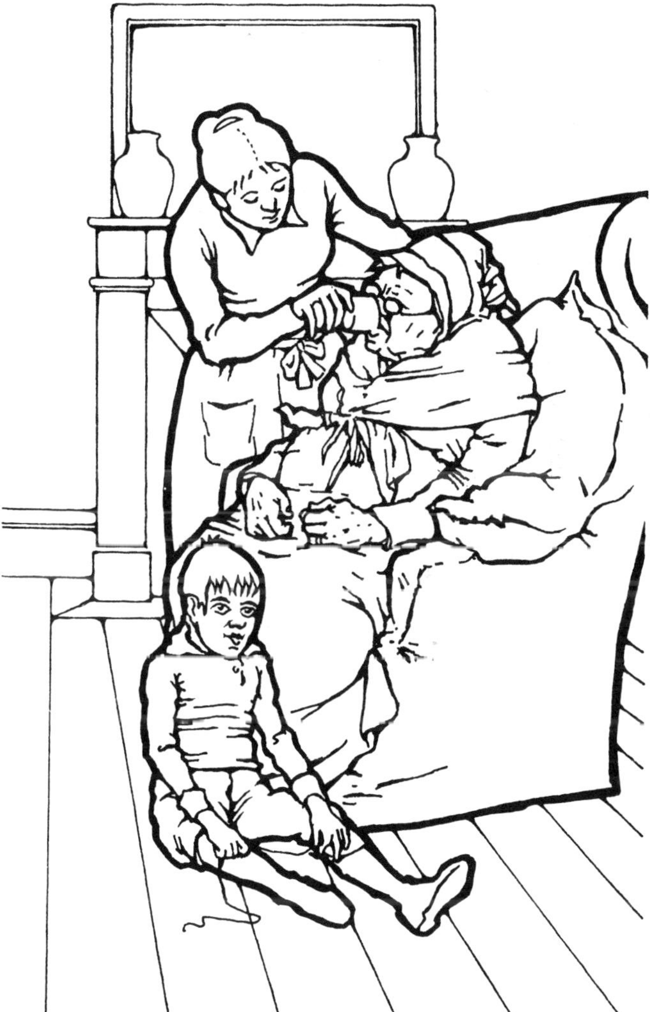

Grandmartini

15. Cautionary and Curative

I had read similar anecdotes and took them as jokes, but Mr Martin Whittome, of Scaynes Hill, Sussex, tells me this actually happened to a friend of his in Austria, where he was travelling with his American mother. She always preceded a meal with a Dry Martini, and ordered her usual tipple with the assurance born of long experience of top bars. But she was in a small village. The waiter, who spoke not a word of English, considered her order but did not query it. He shortly returned and placed three glasses of Martini red vermouth on the table with a defensive 'ein, zwie, *drei* Martini, bitte. . . .'

This does sum up a widespread problem. Americans can take it virtually for granted that in their own country a call for a Martini will produce an adequate Dry Martini cocktail, even if they specify no further particulars. But, elsewhere, this only pertains in grand hotels, bars and restaurants – not always even there. In English pub, French bistro, Italian café – and many other establishments – even if they cater for a good class of clientele, almost invariably a call for 'Martini' or 'Dry Martini' will not produce the required drink. It will be interpreted literally, for in that form it is a widely popular drink. The phrase 'Martini cocktail' is increasingly recognized as indicating a reinforced mix.

In *Wines and Spirits* (Time-Life International) Alec Waugh says that the best Martinis he ever tasted were in Porte's teashop in Tangier. Mr Waugh recalls that opposite this odd Dry Martinian haven there used to be a dress shop run by an American woman. If a customer came in accompanied by a husband, she would suggest the latter relax over a Porte Martini rather than hang about, bored, whilst his wife discussed dresses. Usually, the woman would be unable to make up her mind between two gowns. The husband would be recalled, and frequently would insist his spouse took both. Such exceptions as Porte's to the general rule only emphasize my point.

Many provincial cities of considerable importance in Europe and other continents, beyond the U.S.A., unless they are regularly patronized by American visitors may totally lack establishments with a bartender capable of making even a rudimentary Dry Martini. I regret that in parts of Britain I have come across men masquerading as bartenders, apparently fresh off the boat from distant lands, who have not an inkling what the cocktail is. (Look to see if a pennant of the United Kingdom Bartenders' Guild is displayed or the bartender has a little cocktail-shaker medallion on his lapel: this guarantees at least modest competence.) Many establishments that should be better placed even lack the basic Martini equipment.

The Dry Martinian, marooned in some place where ignorance prevails, must use his wits. In France I have tried 'Martini-gin-with ice'. This may get you a sort of Martini on the rocks, but on not a few occasions I have been served with a glass of red vermouth plus ice, accompanied by a minute liqueur glass of dubious gin. It is best to look at what gin is available and order the best by name: e.g. 'Martini dry – Booth's gin – ice'. Lemon may complicate the issue, unless you are able to describe your requirement in the local patois: 'lemon' – they may be familiar with the alien word – will usually be translated as a round of the fruit or even its juice, not the sliver of peel you need.

In a British pub, if you do not wish to forego your Martini, it's virtually pointless to order it as a mixed cocktail. Ask for a preferred gin, dry vermouth and ice. Then stir it yourself – they may have a spoon handy – and drink it on the rocks. Only occasionally will a slice of lemon rind be a comprehensible request, though – to my fury – they'll put a *slice* of lemon in almost anything unless you order otherwise. Olives are considered an item of rare exoticism. A pub's idea of an onion is a large pickled one: excellent with farmhouse cheese but absurd in a Gibson.

If you happen on an intelligent bar-hand, he may understand a call for a gin with just a touch of dry vermouth – but don't bank on it. You will usually end up with a pleasant gin-and-vermouth, but not a Dry Martini.

Nor, outside the U.S.A., other than in the poshest bars or ones much Americanized, will you get a really *dry* Martini except by spelling out your very precise requirements – in detail. In any event, give the size ('large' or 'double') if you wish something better than a rather small one. Prices vary wildly: there is a fairly broad assumption that all Dry Martinians own oil wells.

After discussing more recondite considerations, when thoroughbred Dry Martinians converge it is likely that conversation will move to that sad condition vulgarly known as the Hangover. There's no denying that Martini addicts from time to time suffer from this 'distressing and almost universal complaint', to adapt the old curative slogan of a proprietary specific against a more epidemic and even more debilitating, malaise.

Since I am professionally involved with spirits, personally I prefer not to admit to the common Hangover, as it might bring discredit on brands I am known to drink. However, should yesterday's Martinis still be with me at breakfast-time the following day, I will admit to sympathizers that I have a touch of E.P.L.: these initials stand for Excessive Product Loyalty – manifestly a meritorious attribute, in principle.

It should be good news for Dry Martinians, whose preferred tipple contains mainly gin or vodka, to know that

Hangover

Dr Gaston Pawan, of the Middlesex Hospital, London, lists these spirits as being the least conducive to the dreaded Morning-After. Dr Pawan is perhaps the only doctor in Britain who has made serious studies of the after-effects of alcohol in a social situation. In 1974 he conducted experiments in which volunteers – I imagine he was not short of them – imbibed 1·5 grams of alcohol per kilogram of body weight. The worst hangovers were, in descending order of badness: brandy (possibly he used ordinary brandy and not cognac); red wine; dark rum; sherry; whisky; beer; cider; white wine – and, least harmful – our two friends.

Intoxication, and consequent distress, caused by Dry Martinis obviously depends on such factors as strength of the gin or vodka, size and number of drinks, degree of dilution, subsequent food and other drinks – and, most importantly, speed of absorption of the Martinis. A leisurely approach is desirable.

If the unwanted aftermath does occur, what to do? No more Martinis that lunchtime for a beginning. Some like to start the day with a Prairie Oyster: a raw egg in Worcester sauce, with salt and pepper as desired, and maybe a touch of cognac – the whole slipped down the throat. (This drink has an interesting origin. It appears that in the Old West, a pioneer was lying in extremis. In his delirium he kept calling for oysters, a commodity unknown on the prairies. A resourceful companion got a wild turkey's egg, poured some vinegar and spirit on it and gave it to the dying man, who enjoyed what he thought was an oyster, and recovered.) It's all a very individual question: I go for Prairie Oysters, Bullshots, Bloody Marys, champagne, and the German specific Underberg – according to time and place. Rest, water and oxygen are perhaps more effective – if more boring – cures.

In any case, a sound Dry Martinian will not often suffer – yet, in a book like this, I've got to acknowledge it *can* happen.

16. Fun and Games: Dry Martini Jokelore

That there are so many Dry Martini jokes and anecdotes is further tribute to the social stature of the drink. Some are adaptations of other stories, some are too ribald for these chaste pages, some are plain bad. Other drinks, other cocktails, simply do not attract this attention. There are even true stories, as when an American visitor was being shown round Booth's great Red Lion Distillery in London's historic Clerkenwell district. On being told how many thousand gallons of gin surrounded him, he gazed admiringly at the huge vats for a few minutes, not knowing how to comment. Then he asked quietly, 'Got an olive?'

That shows how almost inevitably, in such a situation, the mind of a cultivated drinker turns Martiniwards.

Martini stories often come in many versions. I hope that for all readers there will be a few hereafter that are new to them. The most varied, and also the best-known of all, is the 'survival kit' tale, sometimes separated into the 'that's no way. . . .' story. I have heard these related in settings ranging from wartime Britain to the Sahara. It's the daddy of a chestnut and I must include it. I think this combined version is the nearest to the original: an ocean of Martinis has flowed since it was first told. It comes from Mr James Porter, to whom I have previously given credit for obtaining for me the true origin of the Dry Martini.

It can be spun out interminably, but the guts of the anecdote is that the recruit to the Royal Canadian Mounted

Police is issued with a box, only to be opened in the direst emergency. He asks its contents. He is told it holds gin, vermouth, a lemon, a glass. 'What's it for?' he asks.

'It's your survival kit. Supposing you have lost all contact with people; you are hundreds of miles from civilization, you don't know where you are or in which direction to go. You open the box and start preparing a Dry Martini. You won't be lacking for ice. At that moment an American will come from behind the nearest tree and say "That's no way to make a Martini!" '

Another oldie – again there are several editions – in very common currency, I had better get out of the way. It's the one where the bartender is about to press a morsel of lemon peel over a Martini, when the customer halts him, saying, 'When I want a fruit salad I'll order one.'

Now for a few (hopefully) less familiar items of Martini-*memorabiblia*:

Of Dry Martinis:
One is necessary.
Two are dangerous.
Three are not enough.

Mr James Porter has now codified the rules for the Dry Martini game which he gave me for my first cocktail book. It must be played by tired businessmen in an hotel room, preferably on the nineteenth floor or above – away from traffic noise and with plenty of oxygen. The game is played by four men, each sitting at a coffee table on which is one glass and one pitcher containing a pint of 8:1 Martini. Each player has half-an-hour in which to finish his pint of cocktail. At the close of the drinking, one man leaves the room. The remaining players have half-an-hour to guess which one did leave.

Jim also sent me the story of the classicist in a bar:
'Give me a Martinus, please.'
'You mean a Martini, sir!'
'If I want more than one I'll tell you.'

Another from Jim. He says that when a well-known oil company executive (perhaps the story's autobiographical) had sixteen Extra Dry Martinis in a famous Viennese bar and was able to walk out – they fired the bartender.

'Have you heard the latest Dry Martini story?'

Again, there are several versions of this piece of Martini *memorabiblia* – I was wanting to record that word again.

GEN. BOOTH

The man who asked for a Dry Martini in a Salvation Army hostel

Both Mr David Crake, of Glasgow, and Mr Robin Gold, of London, sent me their editions of the following: I print the latter's 'Girl's Lament'.

To drink one Martini I'm able;
Two at the very most –
After three I am under the table,
After four I am under my host.

Two men were sitting at a bar, drinking Dry Martinis. One finished his and then smashed the glass over his neighbour's head. The victim did not react for a minute. Then he said, 'Did you mean that or was it a joke?'

'I meant it.'

'Good! I don't like that kind of joke.'

A chap quietly ingesting a Martini in his favourite bar was distressed that the man on an adjacent stool was gulping down his Martinis at a single swallow. After the third performance he felt obliged gently to remonstrate at this rude application of the greatest cocktail.

'I know it's bad,' replied the drinker, 'but I can't take Martinis any other way since my accident.'

'Oh, I'm sorry; I didn't know that. May I ask what sort of accident?'

'Certainly. I knocked one over.'

This man was watching another Dry Martinian at play. Each time the second man finished his cocktail, before ordering another, he delicately nibbled his glass down to the stem which he placed on the counter for the bartender to remove before replacing it with a freshly filled one. At last the watcher's patience came to an end. 'Excuse me,' he said, 'but I don't understand why you leave the stem. I think that's the best part.'

'The ice melted'.

At a party he met this gorgeous girl in the tightest jeans he'd ever seen. 'Goodness me,' he said, 'how on earth does anyone get into those?'

'You could try me with a Dry Martini for a start,' she said.

Bartenders are never surprised, so when this St Bernard ambled in and ordered a Martini it was instantly produced. The dog drank up and ordered another.

'What do I owe?' it enquired.

'Four pounds,' said the bartender. 'I hope you don't mind my mentioning it, but I've never served a St Bernard before.'

The canine customer eyed him with the mournful glance peculiar to this breed, and answered,

'Judging by what you charge here, I don't suppose you'll ever do so again.'

Sitting on a bench in the central square of a town unfamiliar to him, a man got chatting to a resident. At six o'clock this fellow looked at his watch and said, 'I always have a few Martinis in my favourite bar at this hour. Care to join me?' The visitor accepted happily. When they entered the bar, the resident ordered a Martini for his guest and then the bartender, as by regular practice and unbid, mixed a bumper measure and poured it into five glasses in front of the regular client. This man drank four of the Martinis in pretty quick order and said, 'Well, that's that. Must be off home for dinner now. Nice meeting you.'

'Aren't you going to drink that fifth one?' asked the visitor.

'Oh no, I never touch that one. That's the drink that makes one feel bad in the morning.'

In the quiet English countryside a local duke drove his handsome pony-trap to the door of an inn. He shouted for attention and mine host appeared.

'I require a Martini,' said his Lordship. 'Get a clean bucket, put in some ice, two bottles of gin and a dash of dry vermouth. Slosh it around a bit.'

Well accustomed to the eccentric whims of the aristocracy, the landlord soon staggered out with the mammoth cocktail.

'Give it to the horse,' said the Duke. The landlord did so, and the animal slurped away merrily.

'One for you, your Grace?'

'Certainly not,' replied the peer. 'Can't you see I'm driving?'

The next two tales came to me via Mr Peter Hallas, of The Distillers Company, New York City:

A couple of golfers, waiting for a rainstorm to subside, repaired to the bar and indulged in rather too many Martinis. The sun came out and they staggered to the first tee. One threw down a ball, got out a driver and prepared to swing. Then he stared dazedly at the ground and asked,

'Wish of these four balls should I hit?'

'Suggesh all of 'em,' replied his companion, 'You've got enough clubs in your hand.'

The following episode is said to have taken place in P. J. Clarke's, the celebrated oasis on 3rd Avenue at 55th Street, New York City.

A lady, on her own, sank a number of large Dry Martinis, and then complained to the bartender, 'I'm not having any more of your goddam Martinis. They give me terrible heart-burn.'

'I fear it's not the Martinis, madam. Your left bosom is in the ashtray.'

Stirred – Not Shaken

Mr David McDonald, publisher of the journal of the United Kingdom Bartenders' Guild, reminds me that when the first atomic bomb was exploded in New Mexico, a bottle of dry vermouth in the vicinity was purposefully vaporized. The resultant fall-out was thus minutely, yet decisively, flavoured. Devotees of excessively Dry Martinis believe it is still sufficient to take a beaker of gin and hold it in the open air for the necessary proportion of vermouth to be attracted.

The D.M.N.s – Dry Martini Niggles. Invented by Mary Wallis, my indispensable personal assistant, to describe the querulous attitude sometimes resulting from injudicious (Friday) lunchtime use of Dry Martinis.

For your own
Martini Memorabiblia

General Acknowledgements

Apart from various individuals named in the text, I would like to express, or reiterate, my indebtedness to the following journals: *Gourmet*, *Harper's Magazine*, *New Law Journal*, *Penthouse*, *Playboy*, and *The Spectator*.

In addition, the following books have proved most helpful: *Bartenders' Guide* – (*Trader Vic*, 1948); *Bartenders' Manual* (Harry Johnson, edition of 1900); *Booth's Handbook of Cocktails and Mixed Drinks* (John Doxat, 1966); *Drinks and Drinking* (John Doxat, 1972); *Drinking With Pepys* (Oscar A. Mendelsohn, 1963); *Esquire Drink Book* (1956); *The Fine Art of Mixing Drinks* (David A. Embury, 1948); *The Kindred Spirit* (Lord Kinross and H. K. Humphreys, 1959); *On Drink* (Kingsley Amis, 1972); *The Savoy Cocktail Book* (1930 edition); *Wines and Spirits* (Time-Life, ed. Alec Waugh, 1969).

Endpiece

'You're writing what?' they said.

I told them.

'But you can't possibly devote a whole book to a single cocktail!'

'I can to the Dry Martini,' I replied. But I wasn't, for all my sanguine attitude, all that sure I could.

Now that I have completed my task, I am aware that I may – as happens in actuality to some Dry Martinians – be accused of having fallen between two stools. I have tried to combine ingredients ranging from the profound to the facetious: can these opposites satisfactorily be stirred together? I believe they can if immediate contrast not too violent. That is why I broke the book into numerous parts, leavened with digressions – so that those who were not interested in one aspect of the subject might find information or entertainment in another section. I have aimed at producing a reasonably harmonious entity – but not an innocuous cocktail. I shall have failed if I have not been polemical enough to stimulate disagreement as well as approval.

This is where I must most willingly express gratitude to those who have specially aided me: to Mr Kingsley Amis for contributing the Apertif; to Mr Brian Thompson, who played a crucial part in getting my project off the ground; to Mr Peter Goodchild who collated the photographs and overseas information; to Mr John Chaplin for his brilliantly imaginative drawings; to Miss Mary Wallis, who lent her time to puzzling out my writing and correcting my spelling; and to my wife, Diz, for putting up with me in the throes of aggressive composition. I also owe thanks to Mr Robin Perry and to Mr Clive Greaves.

Except where otherwise attributed, all opinions are mine, and facts, fictions, historical allusions, etc. are published on my own responsibility.

I now commend my work to the *Dry Martinians* of the world.

Royal Borough of Kensington & Chelsea, London